Routledge Revivals

International Politics

Originally published in 1920, *International Politics* provides a general introduction to the subject by looking in detail at the international political situation at the time of writing as well as key issues that frequently appear in these situations. Conclusions are then drawn on which aspects of politics could be improved upon and the function of public opinion as well as providing economic facts to illustrate these points. This title will be of interest to students of politics and political history.

International Politics

C. Delisle Burns

Routledge
Taylor & Francis Group

First published in 1920
By Methuen & Co. Ltd

This edition first published in 2015 by Routledge
2 Park Square, Milton Park, Abingdon, Oxon, OX14 4RN
and by Routledge
711 Third Avenue, New York, NY 10017

Routledge is an imprint of the Taylor & Francis Group, an informa business

© 1920 C. Delisle Burns

All rights reserved. No part of this book may be reprinted or reproduced or utilised in any form or by any electronic, mechanical, or other means, now known or hereafter invented, including photocopying and recording, or in any information storage or retrieval system, without permission in writing from the publishers.

Publisher's Note
The publisher has gone to great lengths to ensure the quality of this reprint but points out that some imperfections in the original copies may be apparent.

The publishers would like to make it clear that the views and opinions expressed, and language used in the book are the author's own and a reflection of the times in which it was published. No offence is intended in this edition

Disclaimer
The publisher has made every effort to trace copyright holders and welcomes correspondence from those they have been unable to contact.

A Library of Congress record exists under LC control number: 20016852

ISBN 13: 978-1-138-18209-7 (hbk)
ISBN 13: 978-1-315-64659-6 (ebk)
ISBN 13: 978-1-138-18212-7 (pbk)

INTERNATIONAL POLITICS

BY
C. DELISLE BURNS

METHUEN & CO. LTD.
36 ESSEX STREET W.C.
LONDON

First Published in 1920

PREFACE

THIS book is intended not for the specialist but for those who wish to have a plain statement of the international situation and the chief problems which arise in international politics. It is an introduction to the subject and therefore contains references to facts which will be quite familiar to many : but even those who know something of the subject may perhaps find it useful to review familiar facts in a new analysis. There are two kinds of introductory study ; one deals with very general statements covering the whole field, the other gives only typical examples and does not attempt to cover the whole field. The latter is the method adopted here. It has seemed better, for instance, to give a few detailed descriptions rather than to attempt a complete general statement as to undeveloped territories or foreign investment. The examples, however, are intended to be sufficiently various to give a fair idea of the complexity of international politics.

Every chapter contains two elements—a description of certain facts and an indication of problems connected with these facts. It should be recognised, however, that this implies a certain view of the subject called politics. Many books on political facts such as government are merely descriptions of organisation and of its working : for to many minds a knowledge of administration means only an acquaintance with the process of administration. Here on the other hand it is implied that politics is mainly concerned with the purposes for which government and administration are supposed to exist : and therefore a knowledge of politics is in the main an appreciation of what there is to be done and only in a secondary way a conception of how to do it. For this reason it has been thought better not to confine attention to a mere analysis of the situation, but to suggest in every case that there might be improvement or at least that the situation is not final or inevitable.

It is outside the province of an introductory study to offer solutions of political problems and, therefore, the whole book is a statement of fact and an expression of doubt rather than the exposition of a doctrine, programme or policy. The need of the general public and even of some statesmen appears to be not so much the inculcation of a gospel as instruction in an alphabet: for ignorance of facts, not ill-will, appears to be the greatest obstacle to progress in regard to international affairs. This, however, does not imply that the book is intended to be quite colourless as regards the solution of the problems described. A certain very definite attitude has been adopted; and certain very definite conclusions are implied in regard to some issues. For example, it is quite clearly supposed that the interest of all nations is not to be found by the ancient process of each seeking its own: and it is implied, without adequate evidence offered here because the evidence is regarded as obvious, that war is an altogether evil institution and a useless political method. Even such assumptions and conclusions need not be accepted by the reader. They are mentioned in this preface simply in order that the reader may be on his guard: for it is considerably better that he should think for himself than that he should agree with the author of any book.

The scheme of treatment, then, is as follows. A description is given first of the governing principle in international politics, the Great Power system and the distinction between different kinds of states or governments: with regard to the state system it is suggested that it gives rise to the problem of the independence of small states and the prevalence of the test of comparative force or wealth. The analysis of facts then involves a reference to different cultures, nationalities, religions and emigrant groups, all of which have their own obvious difficulties. Next the relation of highly organised to undeveloped peoples is shown to give rise to problems of the use of natural resources, settled government and the freedom of the weak. Finally, economic facts are reviewed—governmental action in tariffs, and non-governmental activities such as foreign trade and investment: in this regard the problems are those of international interdependence. Attention is then turned to the organisation which has

PREFACE

been evolved for " foreign " politics—diplomacy and armaments, which give rise perhaps to as many problems as they solve : but the latest stages of international organisation, conferences, bureaux and finally the League of Nations are described as likely to improve on the old methods ; and the book ends with an indication of the function of public opinion and unofficial efforts in removing most of the evils which are to be found in the sphere of international politics.

C. DELISLE BURNS

LONDON

April, 1920

CONTENTS

PART I

DESCRIPTION OF THE CONTACT OF PEOPLES IN GOVERNMENT, TRADE AND GENERAL CULTURE

PAGE

CHAPTER I.—INTERNATIONAL POLITICS AND THE PAST 1

The meaning of international politics. Development of the present situation since the Middle Ages.

CHAPTER II.—SOVEREIGN STATES 14

The Great Powers. Other groupings of the states. The influence of wealth and power in the relation of states : advantages of the Great State.

CHAPTER III.—DIFFERENCES OF CULTURE .. 34

Nationality. Religion.
Social diversity : the migration of workers. Labour and the governing classes.

CHAPTER IV.—UNDEVELOPED COUNTRIES 54

Subordination of minor states and parts of states by industrialised countries : exploitation of territories inhabited by "native" races.

CHAPTER V.—INTERNATIONAL TRADE 78

(a) Governmental action. Currencies : tariffs, etc.
(b) Non-governmental activities. Foreign investment : banks : international companies : shipping : fluctuations of trade.

PART II

DESCRIPTION OF THE INTERNATIONAL ORGANISATION OF THE CONTACTS OF PEOPLES

CHAPTER VI.—DIPLOMACY 119

Foreign Offices and the foreign services. Armaments. International organisations, governmental and voluntary.

INTERNATIONAL POLITICS

	PAGE
CHAPTER VII.—OFFICIAL INTERNATIONAL ORGANISATION	143

Pre-war International Unions. The League of Nations and the International Labour Organisation.

CHAPTER VIII.—UNOFFICIAL INTERNATIONAL ORGANISATIONS 162

International Congresses. Red Cross. Labour Internationals. The Press. Public Opinion and International Politics.

TABLES AND CHARTS

TABLE I.—Wealth of the chief countries in 1914 .. 17

TABLE II.—Imports and exports (1901 and 1912): gross values for certain countries 84

TABLE III.—Imports and exports (1912): kinds of material for certain countries 86

CHART I.—Average dividends of certain railway companies 56

CHART II.—Fluctuations in imports and exports .. 113

CHART III.—International fluctuations in food prices. 115

DIAGRAM: International Metal-buying Combination (1916) 108

INDEX 187

INTERNATIONAL POLITICS

CHAPTER I

INTERNATIONAL POLITICS AND THE PAST

THE average man is not often troubled about foreigners. The Englishman eats the oranges grown by Spaniards, the Frenchman drinks coffee from Brazil or Java; but neither thinks of the foreign peoples whose labour has produced the food he uses, for the commodities of the world are more truly international than are the minds of men. Our clothing, our food and our houses, our railways and our telephones are all international, because the material necessary for making them is contributed by men speaking many different languages and living under many different forms of government: and the internationalism of modern life is not merely material, for the structure of our telephones and even the cut of our clothes is partly due to ideas which have come from abroad. Our medicine and surgery are the results of an interchange of ideas between many nations and no art is so national as to be untouched by foreign influence. The religious, political and social habits we have acquired are due in part to the influence of foreigners; and indeed there is no section of life which is isolated from the action of international interchange.

All this, however, is commonly ignored. The average man no more thinks of the source of his coffee or his medicine or his shirt than he thinks of his digestion—until it goes wrong. When the oranges and the coffee cease to come or when fares on the railways go up because boilertubes no longer are produced abroad, then the average man shows an interest in international affairs; but the character of his interest is like that of his interest in indigestion. He feels aggrieved.

He is offended that the machine does not work: and he

is easily led to suspicion and hatred of what he cannot understand. Therefore the most common attitude towards international affairs is apathy when the machine works and a sort of political dyspepsia when it does not.

The superior person meantime, despising the average man, is often more hopelessly savage, since his passions, being based upon arguments, survive even an acquaintance with the facts. The superior person has a theory about foreigners: either they are deluding us into buying their coffee or their boiler-tubes for their own interest or they are undermining our character by strewing our path with their orange peel. There is, indeed, another type of superior person who regards the foreigner with a benign condescension: but both types agree in thinking of international affairs as a conflict of interests, while the average man does not think of them at all. The facts of international interchange, however, are of increasing importance to the average man; and the chief elements in the present international situation are so recent in origin that our inherited ideas are inadequate to describe the complexity of modern life. An analysis of the facts, therefore, is necessary.

The first requisite for a knowledge of these facts is the attainment of a point of view from which they can be seen. It is only by moving out from his cave that the savage can distinguish a beast from a boulder; and when he has come out of his cave, he will find it convenient not to lie behind one rock all the time nor to climb only one tree. But—what happens at meetings of the representatives of different nations? Each sits behind his own rock or each ascends his own tree and argues violently from his own point of view. The representative of France argues for the Rhine frontier, the representative of the United States argues for the Munroe doctrine, the representative of Great Britain for freedom to blockade: and the result is either confusion or an agreement which covers with meaningless words irreconcilable opposites. In domestic politics, however, another method has been developed. The representative of Muddleborough presents his view of the national interest as a whole, and so does the representative of Little-Puddle-in-the-Bog. They are elected not simply to serve local ends but for the sake of some national policy, which is viewed from different angles but is the same object of vision. There is disagreement between electors and disagreement between representatives; but at least they are

INTERNATIONAL POLITICS AND THE PAST

looking at a common object, whereas at a Congress of diplomatists or at a Peace Conference, each representative looks at a separate interest and the international point of view is commonly regarded as either unpatriotic or out of place. The chief problems of international politics, therefore, arise from an absence of the international mind in the conduct of practical life : and it is not likely that we shall solve any of those problems until we can think habitually of international affairs as we do, in our different towns or counties, of the common interests of the whole nation. The defect is universal. There is no country or people which is now able to take a world-view and consequently no representatives, even if they wished, would dare to take action based upon anything but a more or less enlightened selfishness.

There is, however, a large field in which the international mind might work, without regard to the conflicting interests of the different peoples. All peoples are equally concerned in the increase of available commodities, the improvement of transport, and the development of the resources of the world. All peoples are the gainers if there is an increase in productivity. These statements do, indeed, imply that industry and commerce are not forms of war, and that the only reasonable trade competition is a competition in service ; but the proofs of this need not be given here, for the attitude so expressed is not uncommon among those who think at all on such subjects. It would follow that, so far as economic wealth is concerned, the international mind would set itself to organise the resources of the world for the use of all men. But there is a further step to be made in international politics : for as in the case of wealth so also in regard to order and liberty, all peoples gain from the increase of these. This implies that the representatives of every state in an international congress should desire and work for order and liberty in every other state, but that the understanding of these terms should be somewhat more subtle than when they are conceived by the inhabitant of Muddleborough to be embodied in the habits and customs of his village. As things now stand the words order, liberty and justice are on the lips even of statesmen ; but war is the principle upon which international politics rests and war implies that each people desires in a rival state disorder and discontent, not order and liberty.

Even national interests, however, if selfishness were

sufficiently enlightened would compel attention to international problems. It should be easily seen that the consideration of the resources of the world and their full development in order and liberty are vital interests of every nation ; although it is still imagined by many that the interest of their own nation is best served by the impoverishment or enslavement of other nations, and only the actual effects on themselves of ruin abroad will ever persuade the unintelligent to think internationally. Disease crosses frontiers, disorder spreads ; and impoverishment abroad means smaller markets and more unemployment at home. The political world is, therefore, sufficiently inter-connected over the whole surface of the earth for men to understand that even their own national interests cannot be attained without some consideration of the common interests of all men : and this consideration is a part of international politics. The interests of all are not, however, in international politics understood either in a humanitarian or in a Positivist sense. The idea of human brotherhood or the unity of the human race is too indefinite to be a basis for practical action or even for analytical thought. The different common interests of men, therefore, must be distinguished ; and they must be worked for not merely by the inculcation of good will, but by the discovery of the many different means of attaining them. International interests in regard to non-material "goods" such as justice and liberty depend upon the fact that the more each man or group of men has of such goods, the more there is for others. That is obvious in the case of justice : but liberty needs to be defined and the kinds of liberty distinguished in order to see how each man gains from the liberty of others. With regard to material goods such as food and clothing, it is an international interest that there should be more of them, for what one has another must lack : but it is also an international interest that each man and each group of men should have enough, and policy should therefore aim at some international principle of distribution not the mere "foreign" policy based upon the taking of all by the strong and the lack of all by the weak : for, as in the contacts of individuals so in the contact of peoples, the strong gain most from a system which gives enough to the weak. Such are the principles which affect the international view of the contact between nations.

Before analysing the facts it is necessary to define more

INTERNATIONAL POLITICS AND THE PAST

precisely the kind of facts to be dealt with. Politics may be taken to mean that activity of man which concerns government and parties, law and administration as the means and, as the ends or purposes of action, order and liberty or justice. Politics, therefore, includes all that refers to states or local government and excludes what refers to churches or to the supply and distribution of commodities, which is usually called economics. A part of politics is domestic and a part international, since there is a distinction between the state as a separate unit and the state as an element in the world of states, governments or peoples.

The principles of justice are not different in regard to domestic and international politics ; but their application differs ; and therefore the principles of international justice have to be thought out not in the abstract but in reference to the problems which arise from the contact of governments or peoples. Again, the fundamental interest in domestic and international politics should not be regarded as different, since both should be concerned with men, women and children—the happiness and fuller lives of these, and not the mere instruments—the states, churches and economic organisations, which should serve men. But the happiness of men in terms of domestic politics concerns housing, drainage and education, whereas this happiness in terms of international politics concerns peace and war, foreign trade and national traditions.

The distinction, then, between domestic and international politics may be best understood by classifying familiar ideas. Domestic politics is concerned with such subjects as taxation, local government and electoral methods : international politics is concerned with tariffs, armaments, treaties and the other relationships of states or peoples ; but there is obviously a field in which subjects are to be found which are partly domestic, partly international, as for example, racial minorities, trade regulation and routes of communication.

A distinction should be made between international politics and what is commonly called " foreign " politics, since foreign policy generally means the action of any one state in regard to all others. The common idea of foreign policy preserves just that provincialism of mind which was shown above to be an obstacle to the understanding of international politics : for in foreign policy the accepted purpose is the attainment of a separate interest generally conceived as opposed to all others. To be interested in foreign politics appears to mean to be interested in foreigners and this is often connected with a mere acquaintance with a foreign tongue or a knowledge of the habits or policies of a foreign people. It should be understood, however, that international politics demands a larger view, just as in domestic politics it is not enough to know the idiosyncrasies of the Yorkshireman or the dialect of Somerset. In the first place there are men who can speak seven languages and have nothing of importance to say in any one of them : hence although it is unlikely that a man will think internationally to any effect who cannot think in more than one language, nevertheless a knowledge of languages is no guide to international politics. Secondly, a knowledge of what a foreign nation is like is quite different from a knowledge of *the relation between* any two nations. International politics is not the study of many separate countries but the study of the relation between them. Once again therefore, " foreign " politics is either a bad name for international politics or it is a name for an entirely different subject : but it is difficult to persuade either average men or philosophers to recognise the distinction between saying (1) there are many peoples differing in character and government and saying that (2) each people's character and government is what it is because of its relation to those of other peoples. The second statement is the basis of international politics. The facts, therefore, which are to be dealt with in international politics are all those which affect or are affected by the contact between peoples living under different forms of government. That contact is in the present world very complex and continuous and it is developing in strange ways under the influence of telegraphy, railways, steamships and the completer control of man over the separatism of Nature.

It is a commonplace that the present situation is largely the result of past events. Sometimes this statement is carried too far, when it is assumed to mean that the present is nothing but the surviving past : but even allowing for the entirely original incompetence of men in each generation, they have some ground for looking askance at their forefathers. Some good and some evil now existing, some bad habits and some fine ideals are survivals; and therefore it is necessary to look back before we look round. But in no section of politics does the past survive so obviously as in the international. The lofty sentiments of international peace and a League are old, and so are the atavisms of practical diplomacy. Bombing aeroplanes and submarines are new; but the policies of which they are the instruments are those of Assur-bani-pal and perhaps even of the anthropoid apes who were our common ancestors. The desire for peace and most of the plans for its attainment are old, and so is their ineffectiveness. Omitting the far distant past, the origins of much of our international politics may be found in the Dark and Middle Ages which separate present European organisation from the Empire of Rome. Ideas indeed control us still which come from Athens and Rome, habits which come from Assyria and Egypt: but most of our institutions and social habits arose in the Dark Ages. From the fifth to the tenth centuries of our era the nations and religions of most of the present world were being formed; and the formation of Europe eventually showed itself to be the most important element in international politics. China had its own period of gestation, but its life did not become international until recently and therefore international politics is dominated first by the inheritance of the Dark Ages. When the Dark Ages ended, the assumption upon which the new Europe of the Middle Ages was found to rest was the fundamental community of all the men who counted at all. For five centuries until the fifteenth, therefore, the dominant idea in the contact of peoples was a dimly conceived community of interest. Those who actually preserved the contact, the clergy, the scholars and the kings and knights, were all members of an international caste. Diplomacy, in our sense of the word, had hardly begun. The peoples were indeed more separate than they are now, but they were not felt to be so separate; and the governing classes were less separated by nationality, language or custom than they now are. The commodities in use were local in origin, but the prevailing social ideas and therefore the minds of men were international. Thus a practical community of interest was acknowledged, although its meaning was confined to what then was regarded as the spiritual sphere.

Then came the great change known as the Renaissance. This was fundamental to international politics. Governments were established upon the basis of linguistic or local groupings called nationalities; the governing classes came more closely into contact with their immediate surroundings and the peoples became more conscious of their separateness. For another five hundred years, until our own day, the habits and beliefs were being developed which are now understood by the words sovereign state, nationality, diplomacy and the rest. Separate groups of men in different localities began to experiment with separate and diverse social ideas in religion, education and politics. The minds of men ceased to be dominated by the vague earlier internationalism and the commodities of daily life were still local in origin and use. The past which survives in international politics is chiefly that which lies as far back as the Renaissance. That past is more vigorous in our practices to-day than the Middle Ages, which have become a faded and romantic memory.

In the last five hundred years since the Renaissance, three periods may be distinguished; the first ends with the great international lawyers of the seventeenth century, the second with the French Revolution and the third with the European War, the effects of which still govern the situation. In international politics the first period is the age of diplomacy, the second is the age of the Balance of Power, the third is the age of nationalism and imperialism, sometimes in opposition, sometimes combined. Our inheritance from the first period, the diplomatic system, rests on the conception that the organisation of the relation between governments is best attained by (1) representatives of each state resident in the capital of every other and (2) periodical conferences for specific purposes. Since the relation of governments was essentially one of war or preparation for war and since war is essentially force and fraud, chiefly fraud, the resident representative was at first frankly a spy and his method was professional lying. Hence the definition of an Ambassador as " one sent to lie abroad for his country." The classical descriptions of the prevailing situation are in Machiavelli's *Prince* and Hobbes' *Leviathan :* their conceptions of what *ought* to be done are irrelevant here, but their analysis of fact is unrivalled in the literature of international politics and much of their analysis is applicable to present circumstances. Governments are still in international politics the leaders of armed bands "in the state and posture of gladiators"; the purposes of governments in international affairs are still achieved by force and fraud, and therefore the methods of diplomacy which we have inherited from the first period of modern history are still largely those of the Renaissance world. The period ended, however, with the statement of a common rule for the limitation of force and fraud. This is now called International Law and it has been much elaborated since Hugo de Groot published his *De Jure Belli et Pacis*; but it is still chiefly concerned with war.[1] The common rule which is supposed to control the action of sovereign governments in the international sphere was a great conception. It implies that even in spite of force and fraud the peoples of the world acknowledge a moral criterion in their dealings with one another: and this, therefore, is the good which we have inherited from the first period of modern history.

During the second period the Great Powers of the modern world were gradually consolidated. Spain was declining and France was becoming the storm-centre; Austria and England were establishing heterogeneous empires; and Russia was entering into the European state-system. The action of governments and the methods of diplomacy were rendered easier by the growth of standing armies and professional navies: but the commerce of the nations was creating new problems, for the commodities of the world were becoming international. There was, therefore, a confused struggle for trade in which the governments took part by the use of their always increasing military forces.

The assumption on which the foreign policies of governments was based was that if the contending forces were exactly balanced, no open and destructive conflict would be risked by any party in the international gamble. This is called the Balance of Power, and it is our evil inheritance from this second period. But government meanwhile was becoming more stable, the relations of states less dominated by personal caprice and it was on the whole good that it should be assumed that equilibrium and the maintenance of peace was the chief purpose of foreign policy, although the method used provoked endless war.

[1] It has often been noted that although de Groot's book was supposed to deal with peace as well as war, peace is only referred to in a final and insignificant chapter.

This period ended with the Congress of Vienna in 1815, one of the most ridiculous of all international gatherings. The treaty then signed deals interminably with the frontiers of petty principalities, all of which disappeared ; but it entirely ignores the force of national sentiment, then regarded as Bolshevistic, and establishes forever the principle of " legitimacy," which is now hardly secure even in Siam.

The third period, since the defeat of Napoleon, has been marked by the effects of national sentiment and economic expansion. Both Italy and Germany achieved national unity, Greece and the Balkan nations were freed from Turkish dominion and the Spanish and Portuguese colonies in America became independent republics. There was also an expansion of Europe into undeveloped Africa, parts of Asia and Australasia, which produced the peculiar phenomenon of modern Imperialism. In some cases, as in that of Italy and Germany, the movement towards national unity was the same as the imperialistic movement which led these nations into Africa. The manners and customs of diplomacy in this period were somewhat changed, because of the predominance of economic interests in the industrial system and the close alliance of financiers with diplomatists. The new problems of international politics were those of undeveloped countries, protectorates, spheres of interest, the " open door," sources of raw material and markets for manufactured goods : but uneconomic disturbances confounded diplomacy throughout the period in the Balkans. A first beginning, however, in international politics as opposed to " foreign " politics was made in this third period : for the Concert of Europe and various international Conferences did imply that there were interests common to many nations and that governments should consider these as well as their own separate interests. This third period has ended in the Great War and it is impossible yet to foresee what character the new period in international politics will bear.

Certain general conclusions can be drawn from this history. Diplomacy, the chief method in international politics, had its characteristics fixed in the first period : the chief principle of action, the Balance of Power, was developed in the second period ; and in the third the chief purpose in international politics, control of economic wealth, was dominant. These are as it were the ruling ideas ; but other ideas also were at work though hardly

INTERNATIONAL POLITICS AND THE PAST 11

affecting the actions of state-agents in their dealings with their fellows. Almost independently of the state system, popular passions and political incompetence, the peoples of the world have been brought into much closer and more continuous contact. The third period to which reference is made above (1815-1919) has witnessed a material revolution. Communication has become easier and more rapid through telephones, telegraphs and wireless, as well as railways, steamships and aeroplanes. This has made a great part of the old diplomatic organisation simply ludicrous, since the " principals" now communicate more effectively without representatives : but it has also made the methods of warfare more serious, because more rapid and more destructive. Again, supplies have become more abundant than they were before 1815 ; although this appears not to have improved the quality of life but only to have increased the numbers of the persons living. The populations of the different countries have multiplied, but their prevailing habits and customs have not become more humane. Material wealth is more abundant and the use of it more barbaric.

A second general conclusion is that there has been very little development of thought in the history of international politics. History is often conceived as a mere record of events : but if it is that, it has neither meaning nor value. It is useless to know that one event followed another, unless there is some change to be seen as the years pass in the ideas, customs and conscious practices of men ; but whereas in the political history of any civilised race there is a growth of legislative and judicial systems, new administrative methods and changed habits, so that men, for example, no longer walk the streets armed, in international politics, on the contrary, the methods of savage cunning are still to be found ; and the greatest change seems to be the mere increase in the instruments of force and fraud. Thus the usual history of international or foreign policy is not a record of progressive development of ideals and methods, but a mere repetition by succeeding generations of the most primitive habits of their ancestors.[1] This lack of moral and intellectual development is a deficiency in the peoples of

[1] This is very clear in Emile Bourgeois' " Manuel historique de Politique étrangère," 3 vols., Paris 1892-1906. It deals with the whole world of states ; but it is hopelessly French in its point of

the world; and it is quite beside the point to put the blame upon their leaders or representatives or upon the groups of financiers and traders who have selfish aims. International politics demands a more enlightened public opinion and a more genuine application of moral ideals to the thought and practice of ordinary men.[1]

view. Thus the Middle Ages are said to end when France withdrew from crusading—which is nonsense. Further the book is a study in futile rivalries without any clear perception of an alternative: and yet it is the only book which deals with the history of international politics.

[1] *cf.* Herbert Croly in the *New Republic*, 31st December, 1919, p. 136. "The rescue of the world from the desolation of the war and the redemption of the promise of appeasement placed a strain upon the moral and religious resources of the Christian nations which they were not capable of bearing. The victors were incompetent to extricate themselves with credit from the morass of their victory for the same reason that they were incompetent to avoid their earlier descent into the abyss of the war. They were the spokesmen of an economic, political and social establishment which, although it put forth grandiose pretensions to civilisation, always turned, when strained or imperilled by domestic or foreign dangers, instinctively and helplessly to force as the final arbiter. That is the sober, sinister and decisive truth. Until they recognise it, the democratic peoples will never attain to any considerable degree of liberation. If it is true, it constitutes a sufficient explanation of the calamity of the war and the tragedy of the peace. For generations the European nations had deliberately cherished political designs which were incompatible with the security of their neighbours, and they deliberately agreed to leave the final settlement of these conflicts to trial by battle. The clear implication of this reliance on force for the vindication of national policy is the abuse of force in the event of victory.

"Because of their constitutionalism or democracy the more civilised nations pretend that in the management of their political and social business they do not leave the final decision to force. They are deceiving themselves. While constitutionalism and democracy have ameliorated some of the evils of the arbitrament of force in politics, they have left it in ultimate command. The state, as now organised, is essentially the embodiment of power rather than justice. Its worshippers, when they proclaim and glorify its sovereign irresponsibility, admit this indictment. It must demand above everything else obedience to its own commands, no matter whether those commands are or are not justifiable. It must insist fanatically on law and order—meaning by law and order, not the triumph of moral knowledge, but the ability of the police to enforce obedience. And the commands which the state must insist all citizens shall obey are commands which are intended in nine cases out of ten to secure to the property-owner not only the undisturbed but usually the exclusive and irresponsible enjoyment of his property. It is of the very essence of the prevailing conceptions both of the state and of property that neither politicians nor property-owners are obliged to recognise any except the mildest obligations in the exercise of their power. . . ."

INTERNATIONAL POLITICS AND THE PAST

We now stand at the beginning of a new period, inheriting much good and much evil from the past, but able, if the desire is strong enough, to transform the whole situation. That situation is governed by the various organisations, institutions and social habits which we have so far developed and the problems to be dealt with in international politics can, therefore, be most clearly conceived under the heads which refer to institutions. There are purely political problems arising out of the system of sovereign states and their relation to one another and to undeveloped peoples. There are cultural problems which arise from the distinction between nations, religions or social classes. There are quasi-economic problems which arise out of the contact between political organisations and the systems used for producing and distributing commodities, such as banks, investments, combines and transport agencies.

For dealing with all such problems we have the machinery of diplomacy, congresses, treaties and agreements ; we have a certain amount of inter-state administration, and we have voluntary associations, of which those connected with labour are the most significant.

These facts define the situation as we find it. It is unstable. There may be a drift towards complete international anarchy ; but international politics is practically concerned with finding ways of betterment in order that the happiness of actual men, women and children may be more secure and more continuous.

CHAPTER II

SOVEREIGN STATES

THE primary fact of international politics is the contact between governments, each regarded as supreme in regard to a particular group of persons or a particular territory. These governments are the executive organs of the several states, and, therefore, their action is taken to be the action of the states, while the people governed are supposed, in some sense, to be the state or to be represented by the state. The peoples of the world, then, come into contact through the states and their governments. In legal and diplomatic language all states are equal, since all are equally sovereign; but their equality is as limited in its effects as the almost fictitious equality of the rich and the poor within any state. In fact, all international politics is affected by the distinction between Great Powers and other states; for in practice the Great Powers control the international situation. When their representatives agree, the opinion of the other states is negligible, and when their representatives disagree, the problem becomes only one of the amount of wealth and power on either side among the Great Powers. This situation prevails when the question is obviously international, touching practically all parts of the world; but if the question is local or restricted in interest, the small states of the locality affected naturally have their say. Thus the Great Powers are international organisations either singly or as a group, while the smaller states tend to become satellites of these or are only local organisations.

The Great Powers acknowledged at the end of the war in 1919 were France, Great Britain, Italy, Japan and the United States. Before the war Germany, Austria and Russia were also Great Powers; and although the number is always changing and although there is no formal admission of new powers, there is a kind of tacit international

SOVEREIGN STATES

agreement on the part of all peoples which makes the list of Great Powers at any moment quite certain. It is possible, then, to make out the distinctive characteristics of a Great Power.

A state is recognised as a Great Power when it has predominant military force; and there is a clear distinction in this matter between all smaller states and the group consisting of France, Great Britain, Italy, Japan and the United States; for the armed forces and the military and naval resources of each of these five are clearly greater than those of any other state.

The conception of a state as so much power is primitive, and is connected with the obsolete conception that the essence of the state is the exercise of physical force. This conception, however, dominates the thought of most people to-day. Thus Japan was hardly recognised as a state when the Japanese were known only by their art; but Japan was readily accepted by the majority as a civilised state as soon as her military force was proved effective against China and Russia. Germany, Austria and Russia are not regarded as Great Powers only so long as their military force and economic wealth are below a certain level. The principle, indeed, was announced by M. Clemenceau in his speech at the Peace Conference, when he reminded those who protested in the name of the smaller states that the Great Powers had in fact control of twelve million men under arms;[1] but this means that the Great Power system is based on war or the preparation for war. The idea of war, then, very greatly dominates the international situation.

The Great Powers, however, are also those states which have a greater number of citizens or subjects and a greater amount of economic wealth among such citizens and subjects; and, therefore, from one point of view, the international control exercised by Great Powers is a crude instance of government by a majority. This is not a mere repetition of what has already been said above as to superior force. The rule of the majority is not necessarily based upon superior force, but rather upon the argument that, if every man counts as one and every man is judge of his own interest, it follows that the views of the majority represent the interests of the majority. This, apart from mere military power, has made it impossible in practice to give

[1] January 26, 1919.

equal weight in an international conference to a representative of Norway, for example, who represents only 2,400,000 persons and a representative of France, who represents 40,000,000, or of the United States, who represents 92,000,000. Indeed, it is easily seen from the lists of population that sovereign states cannot be regarded as equal in the same sense as individual men may be.[1] Again, in regard to wealth, both in the amount of capital wealth possessed by the whole group in a state and in the amount per head of population, a clear distinction can be made between the Great Powers and other states. The accompanying table of figures shows (1) the great difference between those above France and those below her on the list; (2) the preponderance of the United States and the British Empire, if all the parts of the latter were included; (3) and the peculiar position of Japan in regard to the poverty of her individual inhabitants.

Again, a Great Power is a state which has interests, either in dependencies, trade or shipping, which are to be found in most parts of the world; and this fact gives the Great Powers an international status which cannot well be granted to small states. In a sense, all Great Powers are empires, containing not only citizens, but also subject races in their dependencies. This, however, does not completely distinguish them from such states as Holland or Portugal, which have dependencies and "world" interests; nor does it quite explain the peculiar international position of Spain, which is almost a Great Power still, although she has few of the world interests of other powers. Again, Norway has a large proportion of the world's shipping, and Switzerland has a large foreign trade; but neither of these are Great Powers. There is, in fact, an indefinite but practical sense in which all States not Great Powers can be called states "with limited interests," as they were officially called at the Peace Conference. A Great Power is essentially a state whose interests in dependencies, investment or trade are worldwide; and it is for this reason probably that they and not other states are called to conferences such as that of Berlin in 1885 or of London in 1909.

---

[1] A list can be found in the Statistical Abstract for Foreign Countries, Cd. 7527, and further details under the various names of States in the *Statesman's Yearbook* for 1920.

TABLE I

WEALTH OF CHIEF COUNTRIES IN 1914

	£1,000,000 National Capital.	£ Wealth per head.	£1,000,000 National Income.	£ Income per head.
United States	42,000[2]	424	7,250[2]	72
United Kingdom	14,500[1]	318	2,250[1]	50
Australia	1,530[1]	318	258[1]	54
Canada	2,285[2]	300	300[4]	40
Germany	16,550[2]	244	2,150[1]	30
France	12,000[3]	303	1,500[2]	38
Italy	4,480[3]	128	800[4]	23
Spain	2,940[4]	144	230[4]	11
Japan	2,400[4]	44	325[3]	6
Argentine	2,400[3]	340	—	—
Belgium	1,200[2]	157	—	—
Holland	1,050[3]	167	—	—
Sweden	940[3]	168	—	—
Switzerland	800[4]	205	—	—
Denmark	500[4]	176	—	—
Norway	200[4]	90	—	—

[1] Estimate not likely to be inaccurate by more than 10 per cent.
[2] Estimate not likely to be inaccurate by more than 20 per cent.
[3] Estimate not likely to be inaccurate by more than 30 per cent.
[4] Estimate may be inaccurate by more than 40 per cent.

This table is taken from Dr. J. C. Stamp's paper in the "Journal of the Royal Statistical Society," July, 1919; but the order of countries is changed.

A further and more subtle point may be made in distinguishing the representatives of Great Powers from those of other states. Not only do they represent greater numbers, but they are part of a more extensive organisation, and they are, therefore, more accustomed to think and act in regard to large issues ; but international politics generally concerns large issues, and therefore a natural advantage accrues to those who are familiar with the methods and the policies of a modern Great State. Hence sometimes the representatives of small states willingly give place to men trained in the politics or administration of a Great Power, without any intention of deferring to mere wealth and power. It is reasonable to suppose that a man familiar with the complicated machinery of government, for example, in Great Britain will be more ready to grasp international administration than one who is accustomed only to the simplicities of Costa Rica ; and this by no means implies any right or desire of Great Britain to rule the affairs of the world. Of course, exceptional men may be found in any state, and a certain fineness of quality may be found more frequently in the dominating personalities of smaller states ; but in knowledge of organisation and administration the advantage lies with the citizens of larger units. Many arguments may be urged against the Great State. Its citizens are irresponsible, its agents autocratic, its action inhuman ; but it is an advantage to have one type of administration which is effective over a large area, as in the Great State ; and what is chiefly needed in international politics at present is not so much humanitarianism as ability to devise and to carry out action on a world-wide scale.

The distinction between Great Powers and other states has been made even more extreme by the results of the recent war. It was always implicit in that distinction that the governments of Great Powers were freer and more sovereign than those of smaller states. It is now clear that the same principles are not applied in practice to the action of these two distinct groups. For example, the small states of Eastern Europe have signed treaties allowing (1) special protection to racial minorities within their borders, and (2) an appeal of such minorities to the League of Nations ; but no such rights are given to minorities within the frontiers of a Great Power, as in the case of the negroes in the United States and the Irish in the British

SOVEREIGN STATES

Empire; or if it be held that these are not involved in the war settlement, then what of the racial minorities in Alsace and Lorraine? Again, even in earlier times the fortunes of smaller states were decided by the representatives of greater states; but now the smaller states are not even consulted in the making of decisions, as, for example, Rumania and Czecho-Slovakia were not consulted before the terms of the Austrian Treaty were decided. Finally, in former years international organisation, such as it was, was based upon the equality of states, as in the case of the Hague Conferences or the Postal Union; but now the Council of the League and the Governing Body of the Labour Office quite frankly give special status to those states which are Great Powers. It should also be noted, however, that there appears to be a limbo intervening between the heaven of the Great Powers and the purgatorial state of smaller states, in addition to the outer hell for offensive or obnoxious governments. Italy, for example, appears to be a Great Power only for certain purposes; and the limitations of her greatness appear to be due to her economic position, since she is more dependent upon external peoples than are other Powers. She was not given an equal place in deciding the terms of treaties at Paris, when Great Britain, the United States and France were replanning the world. Again, the position of Japan appears to be doubtful, because of her distance from the chief battle-fields, and perhaps owing also to her own abstention. France, again, may be in limbo before many years have passed; and some believe that she is there now, since her economic position and her declining man-power may make a difference to her international status. If this tendency continues, there will be a triple grouping of States—the Great Powers, Great Britain and the United States, deciding the fate of all peoples, giving partial consideration to the Middle Powers, Japan, France and Italy; while these five manipulate with a moderate consideration for prejudices, the international affairs of all other States.

The Great Power system in international politics has been used as (1) the basis for neutrality of certain small states. The neutrality of Switzerland was guaranteed at Paris, November 20th, 1815, by Austria, France, Great Britain, Prussia and Russia; and the same powers guaranteed the neutrality of Belgium in 1839, and of

Luxemburg in 1867. In the last case Italy was invited to be a party to the guarantee, and was thereby raised to the status of a Great Power. Secondly, the Great Power system has been used as (2) the force for controlling the Near East and Africa. In 1856, after the Crimean War, Austria and Prussia were called in for the settlement, although they had not been belligerents; and in 1878 all the other Great Powers forced themselves upon the conference to arrange the Russian-Turkish peace. The list of Powers was increased when in 1884 the United States were represented at the Berlin Conference for regulating trade and government in the Congo districts; and thus it is seen a Great Power is represented at an international conference whether or not it has direct interest in the subject. The third use of the Great Power system is (3) in devising world organisations, as, for example, at the Hague Conferences. The list of seven Powers was added to for the first time in 1907, when Japan obtained the right at the Hague Conference to be represented on the International Prize Court. The number of Great Powers, then, had been increasing before the war, and a section of international affairs tended to be organised by conferences of the Great Powers.

The recent European War has somewhat changed the situation, for three Great Powers disappeared—Germany, Austria and Russia; but the war has not destroyed the Great Power system. Indeed, the Treaties devised at Paris were admittedly dominated by the opinions of representatives of the Great Powers. At one time the four Powers—France, Great Britain, Italy and the United States, but generally only the three—France, Great Britain and the United States—dominated the reorganisation of the world. Japan had the only other controlling voice. It is obvious, however, that the representatives of these states were not more competent than those of smaller states, nor were their peoples more intelligent. They dominated largely on the primitive ground of superior force and wealth, and perhaps also upon the more dimly appreciated ground that they had larger populations and more widespread interests.

International politics, then, is fundamentally affected by the Great Power system, which makes the quasi-legal sovereignty of states appear largely fictitious. It is true that sovereignty still implies a certain independence of a

SOVEREIGN STATES

single government in regard to its own citizens or subjects, and this independence is granted in most cases to all the forty or more states which are now usually represented at an international conference; but the Great Powers exercise much more influence in international politics than that of the governments of the several smaller states, and this undoubtedly limits the external sovereignty of smaller states.

The system is not the creation of diplomatists nor of sinister interests; nor is it the result, any more than it is the cause, of the policy known as the Balance of Power. Its origin is ancient and its causes are complicated. As it now stands, it is the most striking fact of the international situation; but not necessarily the most significant for the future. Its strength is the strength of a rather brutal simplicity; its weakness is the weakness of the governments which maintain it, and that, again, is due to the weakness of intellect and imagination among the peoples who acquiesce in such governments. Political thought and action has not been much devoted to the organisation of the relation of states, and, therefore, such organisation as exists is still based largely upon comparisons of force, wealth or the mere counting of heads.[1] It does not, however, follow that any substitute for the Great Power system can now be used as a basis for international politics; still less does it follow that we must or can accept as a practical principle the equality of sovereign States. A world of small States might be still more primitive if Great Powers were destroyed; and a world in which small states having few citizens could outvote and dominate a few great states with large populations would be obviously fantastic. It is a fictitious idealism which attempts to make the world better than it is or different by the simple process of supposing that it is different or that nothing could be worse.

The bases of the Great Power system have so far been described and examples have been given of both good and bad in the working of the system. It remains to make an assessment of the effect of the action of Great Powers, either singly or as a group, in regard to smaller states. At first sight the system perpetuates a rule of force in the contact of independent governments; the will of the stronger seems to prevail, and this seems to urge the smaller states to military and economic development.

[1] *cf.* The argument in Ch. I, of my "World of States."

The government of a small state may well argue that greater military strength will give its people more control over their own fortunes ; or it may argue that its true safety is to set its greater neighbours to destroy one another or to devote most of their attention to planning such destruction. Again, the government of a small state may become simply dependent upon the judgment and policy of the government of a Great Power. Examples of all these are to be found in the policy or status of Belgium, Holland and South American republics ; and the situation is sufficiently well known to need no further description. The difficulty is that if a government's policy is dominated by that of a foreign government, the people of the small state are really being ruled by the people of the great state, and it is a case of the rule of a majority where the minority have no vote or power at all.

A solution of the problems arising from the Great Power and small state system is out of place in a mere analysis of the situation ; but it may be said that the solution must be based upon developing, not destroying, the system.[1] We must look in the direction of a much more complex international organisation of the state system as a whole. Polities or groups of states may be even now growing up, combining small states for international purposes in federations, or combining small states with different Great Powers, not as alliances, but as administrative organisations for particular purposes and cutting across the too simple distinction of all Great Powers from all small states.

The smaller states are not, indeed, a homogeneous mass of undifferentiated units. There are already important groupings among such states. Among European states, for example, there is a Scandinavian group, which is based upon racial or linguistic likenesses. Norway, Sweden and Denmark have each their own rivalries ; but they have been led to make common arrangements as to currency in the past, and they have now a common organisation for the study of labour problems. They are not unlikely to make common cause in some issues ; and they may find Finland also in agreement with their common policy. One of the most interesting facts of international politics

---

[1] A very unwise scheme has sometimes been suggested of *etats tampons*, or buffer states, by which small and weak states should be established between the frontiers of Great Powers, but this would perpetuate all the worst features of the present system.

SOVEREIGN STATES

occurred in Scandinavia when Norway separated from Sweden in 1905 and became a sovereign state without war, by the will of its people and with general consent; thus proving a certain development of political intelligence in Scandinavia not always to be found in Great Powers when self-determination is in the air.

It is too soon to speak of the grouping of Baltic States and of the international position of such a group, but clearly Esthonia and Latvia may make another group connected either with the Scandinavian group or with Poland. The governments and policies of this part of the world are still too fluid for general comment; but the whole situation obviously depends upon Russia. In regard to Poland, it has been well said that " unless her great neighbours are prosperous and orderly, Poland is an economic impossibility with no industry but Jew-baiting." [1] Czecho-Slovakia may be connected with Poland. It has a German minority and a larger Slovak minority, facing rather than united with the old Bohemia. There are industrial districts working at glass and textiles, and the civilisation is old and stable.[2] The country is, however, an economic fragment and the internal administration as well as the external policy are untried. The Treaty, however, which gives the new state international position may be taken as an example of what is the present practice. The will of the peoples is given in the preamble as the ground for independence and the actual exercise of sovereignty as a further ground. But conditions are laid down by the other states " recognising " the new state and the Annex to Article 20 gives a list of international obligations into which a sovereign state should enter.[3]

The grouping of states in South-Eastern Europe used before the war to be referred to under the general subject of the Balkans; but the position is more complicated now, and at the moment it is not possible to say what groups of states will be formed. Clearly, however, the East European state system is a distinct phenomenon. Rumania, Bulgaria, the Serb-Croat-Slovene State and Greece are grouped together not only on the map, but by history, mentality and governmental status. The fundamental

---

[1] Keynes, " Economic Consequences of the Peace Treaty," p. 273.
[2] It is said that many Austrian industrial concerns were removed into Czecho-Slovakia for greater security.
[3] Cmd. 479, Treaty Series No. 20, 1919.

fact in some of these states is the primitive savagery of the populace when roused. The Serbs and Montenegrins earned themselves some notoriety during the siege of Scutari in 1912;[1] the Balkan Wars of 1912 and 1913 were the occasions of barbaric "atrocities" by all the belligerents.[2] Since the Armistice the Serbs have devastated Montenegro and oppressed its people, and interned a Commission sent to inquire.[3] Further, the position of the government in regard to racial differences is unique. The protest of Rumania against having to promise protection to minorities is well known; and all is not harmony as between the Serbs and the Slovenes.[4] The whole of this group of states is distinguishable as at least peculiar. In South American states government is unstable, but the popular feeling does not appear to run to extreme actions. In Balkan or quasi-Balkan states, however, governments abide or pass in a prevailing torrent of nationalistic and quasi-religious fanaticism.[5] It is indeed difficult, in regard to international politics, to say what problems are solved and what new problems created by the confusion resulting from the Great War; but it is clear that a peculiar Balkan group of states still exists.[6]

The South and Central American states make another definite group. They have their own rivalries among themselves, but the rest of the world correctly classes them together in regard to their form of government, their customs and their economic status. The language and tradition of most are Spanish, but Portuguese in Brazil

[1] *cf.* M. E. Durham, "The Struggle for Scutari," pp. 238, 298. The Serbs killed "enemies" by slow bleeding through bayonet stabs, p. 302.

[2] Carnegie Commission on the Balkan Wars, Report.

[3] *Daily News*, November 22, 1919.

[4] Slovene delegates refused to come to the Congress of Serbian trade unionists in 1919.

[5] Political fanaticism also is prevalent. There are in the new Serbia seven socialist parties opposed to one another, thirteen socialist papers and in the Chamber 140 members are in groups of two or three which will not unite.—*Arbeiter Zeitung*, November 14, 1919.

It is remarkable, however, that Bulgaria has taken the international lead in a new law for the organisation of compulsory social service, not in arms but in factories, mines and fields. The suggestion was made long ago by William James, as a substitute for the idea of state service or military service.

[6] A new group of Caucasian states introduces problems of exploitation or development, since those countries are rich in oil and other natural products. Tobacco factories exist in Georgia, and the Italian Government has entered into the field as a buyer.

and French in Haiti : the intellectual predominance, however, seems everywhere in South America to belong to France. Although a festival of the Race is held periodically in Spain, to express the unity of the Iberian peninsula with its old colonies, the Mecca of South and Central Americans is not Madrid or Lisbon, but Paris. The three great states—Argentine, Brazil and Chile stand out among the whole group; they are known as the A B C states. They speak for South America; they are by far the most wealthy, and have probably the greatest undeveloped resources. A tripartite arbitration treaty—the only example in the world—binds them together; and their relations to the other states of the world are those of equals. Nevertheless, all the South and Central American states are in a peculiar position in regard to other states because of the large amount of foreign investment within South and Central America, which is sometimes unprotected and of which the interest is insecure. Hence European governments have sometimes threatened to use force for collecting debts owed to their nationals. This was a danger to independence, and a doctrine known as the Drago doctrine was therefore expressed by the Foreign Minister of the Argentine of that name. The doctrine was eventually embodied in an international rule in the Hague Convention of 1909. More important, however, than this South and Central American grouping is the connection of all these states with the United States of North America. Of this connection the Pan-American Union is the most potent symbol. The Union was finally established in 1910 at the fourth Pan-American Congress at Buenos Ayres. It has a permanent Bureau and meeting-place in Washington, and the Conferences held there have already done much both to create international understandings in the Americas and to promote the general principles of international organisation in the signing of many treaties establishing Peace Commissions.[1] The unity of the Americas is dependent not only upon physical proximity, but also upon ideas. The republicanism of the rest of America is due to the success of republicanism in the United States; the constitutions of South and Central

[1] *cf. Peace Year Book*, 1911, p. 107, and the general principles of American Peace expressed in President Wilson's speeches at the Pan-American Congress, in " President Wilson's Foreign Policy," p. 102, 154.

America are modelled upon that of the United States; and whatever the dislike of the domineering of the Yankee, the economic life of South and Central America is increasingly influenced by the United States.[1]

This situation is expressed historically in the Munroe Doctrine, which was originally stated in the message of President Munroe to Congress on December 2nd, 1823.[2] It asserted the intention to defend the " political system " of the U.S.A.; to regard the attempt to extend the European "system to any portion of this hemisphere as dangerous to the peace and safety" of the U.S.A.; and to accept the then existing status of colonies or dependencies of any European power. The message also asserts that the United States will not interfere in the internal concerns of any European state. The " doctrine " was explained by the message of President Adams on March 15th, 1826, which showed that it was a " pledge to herself " taken by the United States, and did not involve alliances or military intervention to assist Latin-American states.

The policy thus expressed was in direct opposition to the policy prevailing then in Europe, and the danger of the extension to America of the principles and practices of the Holy Alliance was the real cause of Munroe's statement. The Congress of Verona had agreed to suppress representative government and a free press. In 1820 the people of Naples had ejected their most tyrannous and incompetent king, but the Alliance authorised Austria to send her army to restore him, and this was done in 1821. In 1820 the Spaniards forced their king to grant a constitution; but the Alliance gave leave for France to invade Spain to help the king to repudiate this Constitution, and this too was done in 1823. What would have happened to the revolted colonies of Spain? In December, 1823, Buenos Ayres, Chile, Colombia and Mexico were free; and they and the others might have been reconquered for Spain had not Munroe's statement been made. That is the historical background of the " doctrine "; but the policy

[1] South American thinkers, however, by no means accept the conception of democracy prevalent in the north, as can be seen from the writings of Rodo. Something has been added to international politics by South America in the work of Calvo, Drago and other publicists.

[2] *cf.* A. B. Hart, " The Monroe Doctrine," for documents and later extracts.

SOVEREIGN STATES

expressed in it has been changed and developed, until to-day its results and the meaning commonly given to it would astonish President Munroe.

The fact that the United States did not cease to be endangered by the action of European statesmen after the Holy Alliance had disappeared, is shown by the events of 1861 and 1863. While the United States were distracted by civil war, three European states—France, Great Britain and Spain—combined to attack Mexico. All three landed troops at Vera Cruz in 1861. Spain and Great Britain, however, were soon satisfied, and it was left to France to capture the city of Mexico, which was held by French troops until 1867 as the seat of a nominal Empire. The danger to the United States is the first reason of the policy embodied in the traditional " doctrine "; but it is fair also to acknowledge that it is, as it has been called by United States officials, " a doctrine of peace," for the policy of the United States tends to prevent the rest of America becoming a scene of scramble for power, although it has not prevented small local wars.

The so-called " doctrine " is nothing more than a statement of some fundamental principles of the foreign policy of the United States. It may be allowed for by other nations, but it is not in any sense admitted by them as a principle of international law or practice,[1] although it is acknowledged internationally as the traditional policy of the United States in the Conventions of 1899 and 1907, signed at the Hague International Conferences.

The latest phase of the " doctrine " is its admission into the text of the Versailles Treaty. The article forbidding special understandings is followed by an article to the effect that the prohibition should not invalidate " regional understandings like the Munroe Doctrine."[2] Thus the doctrine is made to cover what used to be called " spheres of influence," and it may be recognised as a principle governing the foreign policy of other states besides the United States of America. The group of American states may therefore be considered to have added two new principles to international politics.

All the groups so far mentioned are formed by states

[1] *cf.* Lord Salisbury's reply to the Olney Despatch, 1895.

[2] Article 21.—The article was apparently inserted by President Wilson in March, 1919, and is believed by some to cover the partition of Asia.

whose governments are in fact independent, but there is a class of states which may be called subsidiary. Even if a certain kind of sovereignty is allowed to them, some powerful neighbour overshadows their external policy. The peculiar position of such states may be understood by reference to the example of Afghanistan. The Afghan dynasty was placed on its throne in 1880 at Kabul by the British; a subsidy was given to the Ameer as a personal gift, and later the Ameership was recognised to be hereditary. By the Convention between Russia and Great Britain in 1907, Great Britain is accepted as controlling the foreign policy of Afghanistan, and it was understood that the British held this control until August, 1919, when the Government of India apparently withdrew its claim.[1] It is not, however, yet clear how the relations of Afghanistan in regard to non-British government will be dealt with in practice by the Government of India.

Another example of a subsidiary state may be found in the case of Panama. Here we see a satellite state actually coming into existence in the orbit of a Great Power. Columbia had control of the proposed route for the Panama Canal in 1903, and a treaty was negotiated between that Government and the United States; but Columbia delayed to ratify the treaty, and a revolution broke out in the city of Panama. On November 4th, 1903, the people of the city declared that they constituted an independent republic and the United States recognised this republic on November 6th, and entered into a treaty with it on December 7th, by which the United States has a strip of ten miles breadth, with sovereign authority over the Canal zone.

Nicaragua is in a still more peculiar position of dependence. The United States have offered money to the bankrupt and discredited government in order that it may pay its debt to American and other foreign creditors; and a body of United States marines for some time controlled the capital city, Managua.

Still more obviously dependent are the three small European states: Andorra under France, Monaco under

[1] Cmd. 324, No. 67. Viceroy backing Sir H. Grant. "By the treaty and this letter Afghanistan is left officially free and independent in its affairs, both internal and external." *cf.* Debate in House of Lords, Hansard, H. L., October 28, November 4, 1919. Lord Curzon said that it was not wise to continue the old system " under modern conditions.'

SOVEREIGN STATES

France, and San Marino under Italy; and there are obviously non-sovereign states, such as Oman.[1]

A special grouping and special problems exist in what is called the Far East. Japan, although normally classified as a Great Power, has the further characteristic of belonging to a far-Eastern group of nations or races, among which she is the most powerful. The mind not only of the Government, but also of the people of Japan, appears to be set upon a domination of Asia, and the Japanese state is peculiar as being the most frankly militaristic among the present states of the world.[2] Japan is also active on the other side of the Pacific, and it was once suspected in the United States that Japan had acquired land in Magdalena Bay, on the western coast of Mexico. During the war, Japanese shipping has become more active than before in the Pacific, and the Panama Canal has made it easy for Japan to send ships to the West Indies. Thus the position of Japan is changing in regard to international politics. The other states of Asia hardly affect international politics, except as passive objects of policy on the part of foreigners, and, therefore, they may be more suitably considered as "undeveloped" countries, in spite of the fact that their sovereignty is not questioned. China and Persia are the two outstanding examples of states within which there is a free play of foreign interests.

There are, therefore, already various groupings of states, and in some cases political organisation of the group has given stability to the sense of joint interests. This is the second important factor in international politics, in addition to the Great Power system; and it indicates a tendency, not to a world-state nor to a further predominance

[1] Apart from states, sovereign or part sovereign, a new position has been created for self-governing dominions of the British Empire. In international politics still the King of Great Britain stands for the whole Empire, but representatives of dominions now sign treaties. For example, in the Convention of September 10th, 1919 (Cmd. 477), regarding the Congo Basin, etc., " H.M. the King " appoints three or four representatives (presumably for the whole Empire) "*and* for the Dominion of Canada, etc." four representatives, and for India one (Baron Sinha). It is interesting that Lord Milner signed twice, once for the Empire and once for South Africa.

A number of new Arab states or Emirates—Hedjaz, Yemen, Asir, etc.—may be found to make a new group: but they may, on the other hand, be divided by attachment to this or that Great Power.

[2] "A Political History of Japan during the Meiji Era, 1867-1912," W. W. McLaren, 1916.

of wealth and power, but to a much more subtle and civilised organisation of international life, based upon a system of polities or groups of states, each organised for a particular region or purpose, and some cutting across the membership of others, since one state may belong to many such polities. Thus the United States is a Great Power in world affairs and also a member of the American polity. Great Britain is an Eastern Government in India, and an Atlantic Government in regard to France and the United States.

The policies of the governments of the several states make up the life of international politics; but it is not easy to summarise the foreign policy even of the most important governments. Certain general statements, however, cover nearly all foreign policy; for example, the political structure of a state, as a democracy or autocracy, makes very little difference to its foreign policy. The fact that the government is controlled by elected representatives does not much affect the character of their dealings with foreign nations; and so a democracy may be "imperialistic"; that is to say, a state in which individual or group liberty is respected, may so act as to suppress such liberty abroad. Alliances between democracies and autocracies are quite possible, as that between France and Tsarist Russia. Again, a nation may have diametrically opposed policies at home and abroad. The French Government, for example, has been anti-clerical at home, but abroad was the supporter of the Roman Catholic Church. Again, in foreign policy more than in any other sphere of state action, administration and executive power still retain their most ancient autocratic form. The reform of legislatures has left the administration still unreformed in most states. It is still believed, even in regard to the home civil service, that the civil servant should be a passive instrument in the hands of the Minister; but in foreign policy this immoral doctrine is still more established, and even the Minister is regarded as the passive instrument of national interests. Thus the states and the governments, which should, if they really worked for justice and liberty, be the best instruments of an international policy, are themselves the greatest obstacles to the growth of the international mind.

Political parties are usually supposed to supply the motive force in state action, but in most countries the

SOVEREIGN STATES

parties do not differ greatly in their foreign policy. Even Labour and Socialist parties, where they have held power, as in Australia or the new Germany, do not appear to have a new foreign policy, although in the expression of general principles they are distinguishable from others. The real trouble is that few persons in any country understand or are interested in international politics, and most political parties regard foreign policy as useless for election purposes. It may be that this is an instance of the hopelessness of the present representative system, in which one man is chosen to represent views on such diverse topics as housing and the treatment of native races ; but whatever the cause, the political organisation of the peoples appear to be either useless or positively obstructive to international policy.

From all this it is evident that the states of the world constitute a problem of international politics and not its solution. Some good is attained by effective governments. Some governments represent the real interests of their people ; some people have a will of their own to be represented. Even the Great Power system is useful. On the other hand, the state system itself is now criticised adversely by vigorous thinkers, and at the very time when, in the early twentieth century, the chief governments of the world seemed to be moving towards the dim beginnings of an international policy, the world has been flung back into barbaric impulses and political reaction. Further, the representatives of the greatest sovereign states are believed by many to have proved themselves so incompetent that it would be fatal to put the affairs of the whole world into their hands. A world-state, modelled on existing states, would be worse than useless.

The problem, then, is how to limit the sovereignty of states so that order shall no longer depend merely upon the will of the strongest, and liberty no longer be sought by the bickerings of the insignificant. Will the new system come from a change in the character of states ? Or will the very fact that the international situation is different, cause all states and governments to be improved ? It is obvious even now that every state is affected by every other ; but if the character and policy of every state affects other states, it follows that any fundamental change in a great state, either in the type of its government or in its traditional policy, will affect the whole of international politics. Already we see new situations being developed in the policy of Great Britain and France, both because of the disappearance of old governments abroad and because of the recent appearance of new states. The Russian Revolution of March, 1917, was followed by the more fundamental change of November 7th, 1917, when the Bolsheviks took power. Thus the Empire of the Tsars no longer threatens India, nor is Russia a free field for the investments of the French banks. On November 9th, 1918, the Revolution in Germany overthrew the dynasties of the old Empire, and on November 12th, 1918, the Republic was proclaimed in Austria. Thus two great armies of the European continent were dissolved, and the power is passing from the landed aristocracy. These are great and obvious changes. But less obvious changes may be no less great. A new mood of any great people, a new international policy deliberately conceived and skilfully carried out, would immediately transform the whole situation and solve the problem of the conflicting sovereignties of armed states.

The present state system, the Great Power system, and the groupings of governments, are parts of a growing and changing life. International politics is not an anatomy of a dead body nor the analysis of a fixed and mechanical world, but the study of a complex and shifting situation of which the elements themselves change as well as the relation between them. Some of the changes are the result of circumstances, over which policy has little control; but some changes are the result of deliberate action on the part of those who desire to improve the organisation of life.

It appears probable from the facts reviewed that, instead of a World State in addition, perhaps, to an all-embracing league and in correction of the older and simpler conception of the equality of sovereign governments, there should be a movement in the direction of developing distinct groups of states. These groups obviously exist already; some of them have the beginnings of inter-state organisation, as, for example, the Pan-American Union; others are closely bound together by the friendship of their peoples or the likeness of their languages and social traditions. If, then, this tendency could be developed into the formation of permanent polities, uniting governments for definite administrative purposes and for limited regions or functions, it might be easier to establish a

SOVEREIGN STATES

genuine international politics in the place of the mere conflict of changing foreign policies. Alliances and Ententes have long been used for the purposes of war and the preparation for war; but little use has been made of joint action between governments for the promotion of justice and liberty and the other goods for which governments are supposed to exist. The majority of men are not yet able to understand world interests and an all-embracing international organisation, but they could easily understand and appreciate the joint action of two or more governments for restricted and defined common interests. Such groups of governments might then more easily be federated or organised in a single system; and the equality of the groups would be less fictitious than the equality of sovereign states. The danger is a new balance of Powers; but if each group existed for joint administrative action and without any common military policy, in the relations between the groups comparative military force would be irrelevant.

CHAPTER III
DIFFERENCES OF CULTURE

THE contact of sovereign governments and the grouping of states is complicated by differences of nationality, race and religion, and by the contrast of social classes. All these different factors in international politics are classed together here as cultural, because culture appears to be the best general term to cover that complex of language, religion and moral tradition which we call nationality, as well as to indicate the characteristic differences which appear in the contact of peoples in emigration or the contrast of social classes. The problems of international politics change somewhat from generation to generation; for example, in the sixteenth century, religion was a much greater source of difficulty than it now is; and in the nineteenth century, emigration was a much more difficult problem than it ever had been before. It is not possible, however, to review here the history of cultural problems and, therefore, all that will be attempted is a description of the present situation.

Problems of Nationality.—The first important fact is that men of different nationality are in contact. No difficulty would result if people speaking different languages or following different customs could live together as amicably as in some countries people do who differ in religion; and perhaps the antagonisms of nationality will subside in more civilised times than ours, as the antagonisms of religion already have subsided except among savages and theorists. Meantime, however, national divisions make men unhappy, both within the frontiers of a state which includes more than one nation and across the borders of states when national passion runs to " expansion."

In many countries or districts different social classes belong to different races or nations or religions, and the problem of nationality is therefore complicated by an economic problem of wages or social status. This was the

DIFFERENCES OF CULTURE

case in parts of pre-war Hungary, Galicia and Germany. The re-arrangement of frontiers has modified the problem in these cases; but the same problem still exists elsewhere.

An example of the connection between national and economic problems may be found in Upper Silesia, which is to have a plebiscite under the Peace Treaty (Article 87). The country contains a large iron and steel industry centred in the Königshütte district. In Chorzow and Zaborze are large electricity works and there is a certain amount of the linen industry. Upper Silesia has been under Prussian rule since the fourteenth century and has been governed from Breslau; the companies controlling the industries are German, and working conditions are not different in the municipal enterprises, which were also dominated by the German managing class. The industrial population, however, is almost entirely Polish in speech and sentiment, and Roman Catholic in religion.[1] The workers have, therefore, never been organised in the trade unions of Germany and there have been very few strikes before the war; while their Roman Catholic sentiments were controlled by the fact that the bishopric at Breslau has been strongly German. The ordinary clergy may, however, have been anti-German, especially since Hoffman rattled his sabre in Poland in a *kultur* policy which was anti-Catholic in order to be anti-Polish. The products of Upper Silesia have hitherto tended to go to Breslau and Berlin. The coal used in Berlin came largely from Upper Silesia. The food of the Polish workers, however, before the war, used to come, by special arrangement of the German government, from Russian Poland. A large importation of Russian pigs used to be common and the people also ate dogs.[2]

Here then is a district in which the nationality of the majority is of one kind, while another nationality has developed all its resources;[3] and upon this national minority have depended the government and industrial organisations of the district, so completely that it may be difficult to make the railways lead elsewhere or change the markets while the capital remains in the old hands. The hostility of ill-paid

[1] German Press of March 10, 1919, etc., summarised in *Foreign Press Review*, March 27th, 1919.

[2] *cf.* Board of Trade Enquiry, 1910, German Towns, Cd. 4032, on Königshütte.

[3] Indications in Cmd. 54, Report of Conditions in Germany, April, 1918.

and oppressed industrial workers towards their employers is here entangled with the hostility of the Poles to the Germans; and the problem of different nationalities in contact is complicated by social and economic differences.

The problem of nationality, however, is best understood when it is not so complicated by other differences, and to this simpler form, therefore, attention must be directed. The most prominent force in international politics during the nineteenth century was nationalism. This resulted in the establishment of the kingdom of united Italy in 1870; in the breaking away from the Turkish Empire of the new Greece in 1832; and in the acknowledgment of full sovereignty for Rumania, Serbia, Montenegro, and Bulgaria in 1878. The same force finally broke up the Austrian Empire in 1918. But the problems of nationality are not yet solved, and they may take on new forms in the near future. In Czecho-Slovakia, a population of 5,750,000 Czechs has control of a non-Czech population of 7,750,000, made up of Slovaks, Ruthenes, Poles and Germans. In the Southern Tyrol, under the secret treaty between Italy and Great Britain, about 250,000 persons come under Italian rule, of whom 70,000 are Italian and the rest German. Unfortunately the peoples of western Europe and of America do not appear to recognise the vitality and importance of what is called national sentiment, since the majority of those who live under long-established governments, and who are not oppressed by men of another tongue, usually mean by the " nation " the groups of men under a distinct government and nationality among them is only a vaguely felt sentimental bond. The Frenchman, Englishman or German feels the pull of nationality, but not in so absorbing an experience as is felt by the Serbian and the Pole. Nationality, therefore, for the purpose in view here needs to be defined; and it will suffice if it be understood that a nation is a group of men, women and children united by blood, language and tradition and having some special association with a particular country.[1] Nationality is the

[1] This is more fully explained in my " Morality of Nations." In U.S.A. some writers imply that " nation " means " the state in its external aspects "; but this is because of the common use there of the word " state " to mean only a part of the sovereign state. Again, " international " Law really means " interstate " Law. Lord Bryce, in his " South America," takes nationality to mean an unorganised nation.

DIFFERENCES OF CULTURE

quality in these persons which distinguishes them from others, and nationalism is the enthusiasm for the nation usually developed into a programme for attaining independent government. Thus nationalism appears chiefly as a gospel of revolt against oppression ; and it is, therefore, in a sense, a domestic problem, since it is an attack by subjects levelled at a sovereign government. An appeal is, however, often made to foreign sympathy, as in the case of Garibaldi against Austria in Italy, Kossuth against Austria in Hungary, and the Greeks against Turkish rule in Greece. This appeal sometimes involves a foreign government in action, as in the case of the Cuban revolt against Spain leading to the Spanish-American war. An example of the difficulty in distinguishing a problem of nationality which is domestic from one which is international, is to be faced in the case of Ireland. It is difficult to say whether such a problem can remain domestic, having in view the interest of the large Irish-American population of the United States. With regard to other nations, as for example the Egyptian, the problem is obviously not altogether domestic, unless Egypt is placed in the same position as India in relation to the government in London.

The most obviously international of the problems of nationality, however, are those connected with the rivalries of nations which have already attained their independence. This is the "sacred egoism" which has been the confessed policy of an Italian party ; and it is not very different from the appetite for "painting the map red" which is to be found among some of the British or the gospel of militaristic dominance preached in Japan. The belief in the excellence of our own nation easily leads to the desire to govern other nations—of course, for their own good : and thus nationalism develops into nationalistic imperialism. The sentiments due to a common tradition among the members of a nation is thus used not as a source of protest against oppression, but to excuse the oppression of other nations : and this appetite for domination appears to be common even among the peoples of those countries which are usually called Christian and civilised.[1]

---

[1] A peculiar version of the same movement is known as Pan-Turanianism, a Turkish national movement which was at first literary, like Pan-Islamism, but was used by the Committee of Union and Progress (Young Turks) as a political force. It aims at

The most fantastic element in nationalistic imperialism is the reference to the past: for example, the German Emperor was inspired by the thought of the Holy Roman Empire of the Middle Ages, although the connection was not easily seen; and the present inhabitants of Rome and even of other parts of Italy took Tripoli and expect Dalmatia because the old Romans once ruled there.[1] On such grounds the Greeks might claim Sicily and the Egyptians part of Syria. The reasoning is politically nonsense; but it is effective with the ill-educated; and in politics what people believe is even more important a fact than what is the truth.

A somewhat wider aspect of the same problem is the contrast between races, understanding the word race to mean a group of nations or tribes with distinguishable physical characteristics, colour or shape of features. Thus the white race is usually distinguished from the yellow and the negroid: and there are also distinctions between Indians, Malayans, Arabs and others. These distinctions are sometimes made the basis for conflict and sometimes these conflicts result in international difficulties. The negro problem in the United States and the racial problems of British India may be supposed to be domestic, although even these have their international reverberations.[2] The more obviously international problems, however, may be

the reunion of Turks; the one million in Kazan, two millions in the Caucasus and the thirteen millions in Central Asia who speak Turkish (Bashkirs, Kirghiz, etc.), besides the Turks in Anatolia.

[1] A small but powerful group in France adopt the same pseudo-historical basis for aggressive nationalistic imperialism. For example, Gabriel Hanotaux in his new book, "Le Traité de Versailles," argues that the Germans are only a group of tribes, not a single nation; and that France should dominate Europe since it did so in the past. In "Come Siamo Andati," etc., p. 107 seq., Professor Salvernini shows up the fantastic history of nationalist Italians.

[2] E. G. Murphy in his two books, "The Basis of Ascendancy" and "The Present South," deals admirably with the negro problem and gives suggestions which may be useful in international politics and the treatment of undeveloped peoples. The position of Liberia in regard to the U.S. Government is of international importance. There are about 10,000,000 negroes in U.S.A., there are associations for promoting joint action with negroes in Africa, e.g. the Hamitic League of the World, the Universal Negro Provident Association, etc. Newspapers such as the *Boston Guardian* represent the same interest.

Sir Alfred Lyall, "Rise and Expansion of British Dominion in India," gives indications of the racial problems there.

DIFFERENCES OF CULTURE

seen in such an anti-foreigner movement as the Boxer Rising in China in 1900. Long experience of foreign aggression, the destruction of the Summer Palace by the barbarian French and British in 1860, the loss of territories to European Powers, the suspicion of missionaries and foreign traders, led to action by a secret society called the Harmonious and Peaceful Fists. Some support was given by the Chinese Government : European churches and residences were destroyed and in the North-West Provinces there was a general massacre of foreigners. A joint international expedition under the German Count von Waldersee marched into Pekin and exacted punishment ; but did not increase the love for foreigners. Reciprocal feelings of European against the " yellow " races exist in North America and Australia. In California there are obstacles to Japanese immigration ; and the Australian Immigration Acts, although they do not exclude any race by name, allow of administrative discrimination which is well known to be directed against Japanese. Here then are tendencies which are obviously important in international politics and of which the view taken even by the two parties immediately concerned should be international, although it usually appears to be based upon the sacred egoism of each party.

Religious Problems.—Religious differences also affect international politics. Until the eighteenth century the relation between European governments was very much influenced by religion. The very earliest times do not concern us here, except in so far as primitive habits may have survived ; but it is as well to remember that the earliest bond of groups within which government developed, was religious. The king was once a religious rather than a political figure : although perhaps it is not possible to distinguish the religious from the political in those earliest societies. The religious bond between men of the same group, whether alone or in combination with other bonds, resulted in a religious attitude towards foreigners. The foreigner was sometimes regarded as an outcast and groups of foreigners as devils or the servants of devils. The idea of a chosen race was widespread in early times and nearly every imaginative race can be shown to have regarded itself as " chosen." These appear to be amiable vagaries when they are read of in history : but their survival in modern times creates a problem of international politics, for many men still feel an atavistic religious horror of what is foreign. Primitive religious oppositions, after the religious "unionism" of the Middle Ages, revived in the controversies of Protestants and Catholics and their effects are recorded in the history of the wars of religion: these also are ancient history, but the results may still be seen in such countries as Ireland or Albania. The general effect of religious passion may, however, be omitted here, and attention confined to a few of the most typical religious issues affecting international politics.

The most important religion for international politics in Europe is Roman Catholicism. It is highly organised and has a long quasi-political tradition :[1] it has moreover, what many other forms of Christianity lack, a definite and not altogether subservient view of the sovereign state. It is therefore often important for a government to know both what the policy of the Vatican is and also what is the prevailing opinion among Roman Catholics.

The policy of the Vatican was, for some time under Leo XIII, tending to liberalism. The Encyclical "Immortale Dei" expressed a benevolent if somewhat antiquated view of the nature of authority in civil matters : but since that time the Vatican has not given any clear pronouncement as to political theory or practice. The most important influence of the Vatican at present is in the support it gives to any group or government favourable or likely to be favourable to Roman Catholicism : and the support of the Vatican involves the use of religious teaching or religious enthusiasm for this or that purpose. Not only peasants but a certain type of educated and æsthetic society are the willing instruments of the policy. The Vatican, therefore, sometimes must be reckoned with as a power in international politics. It gave support to the Italian Government in the Tripoli War, it supported for many years the shaky throne of the Austrian Emperor and it is believed to be on good terms with the military juntas of Spain.

Apart from the effects of direct influence from the Vatican, Roman Catholicism creates international problems by influencing the policy of certain groups, both

[1] There was recently and perhaps still is a College in Rome where priests and students were specially trained in Diplomacy. The extra-territorial rights of the See of Rome, now resting on the Guarantees of the Italian Government, are of international importance.

DIFFERENCES OF CULTURE

socialistic and monarchic. The Centrum Party in Germany, being Roman Catholic, modifies the Socialism of Germany in the direction of authoritarianism tinctured by benevolence. The Christian Socialists of Hungary have a very vigorous and mediæval anti-Jewish policy. Roman Catholics, chiefly Irish and Italian, are organised politically in the United States on a religious basis,[1] and Roman Catholicism colours the view taken of education in the whole of South America. Rumours and ancient prejudices obscure the facts and it is quite impossible to suppose that Roman Catholicism, either officially or unofficially, is nowadays anti-national or destructive of existing governments. But the existence of a large group of men, women and children following Catholic practice and tradition creates problems both within states and across their frontiers. Thus the policy of the French Government for many years although anti-clerical at home has strongly supported Catholic missions abroad, and France has claimed to be the protector of Christians in Asia Minor. Indeed it has been noted in the Chamber of Deputies that France was a patron in Syria of the very religious congregations which she obstructed at home.[2] The forms of Christianity recognised commonly in the East do not bear much resemblance to Protestantism and therefore Christianity there means Catholicism or some other early religion and the word for a western Christian " effrengi " is in fact a corruption of " français."

In Germany and Austria another definite example may be found of the political importance of Catholicism. The memory of the *Kulturkampf* still rankles in the minds of the German ecclesiastics. They have therefore a suspicion of state action, especially in regard to education ; and that suspicion influences great numbers of the workers in the Rhineland and Bavaria. Secondly, the Socialist party for many years before the war was vaguely connected with " atheism," on the ground, held by all ecclesiastics, that anyone who thinks for himself, thinks wrongly. Thirdly, there was a natural alliance between the old monarchist classes and the ecclesiastics : the institutions for which

[1] When the Congo Reform Association attacked a good Catholic the King of the Belgians, because of Congo atrocities, this was taken by Cardinal Gibbons in U.S.A. as hostility to the Church, and the Reform Association was at first opposed in U.S.A. by good Catholics.

[2] L. Marin, Rapport, December 22, 1913.

both stood were mediæval and the fundamental idea of authority is the same in the political, social and religious spheres.[1] All this makes of Catholicism in Germany, Austria and Hungary a very important influence as regards international politics. No one can foresee in which direction that influence will be used : it may be pacific as well as reactionary, but it may on the other hand find alliance with the possessing powers even in a Socialistic state or it may " consecrate " the sword as it has done often in the past, and as appears to be possible in militarist-clerical groups in France. Christianity as a whole may be counted as one religion by contrast to Islam, Buddhism and various African religions ; and a very peculiar religious contrast arises in such countries as Armenia and Macedonia. Here the religious difference is complicated by racial and sometimes economic differences, but yearly religion here is an important factor in international politics. The Armenians, for example, profess a for of Christianity and appeal on that ground for the sympathy and even the military aid of Russians and English against Turks and Tartars.[2]

Another religion of international importance is Judaism, although in this case the binding idea of the group is almost as much racial or national as it is religious. Judaism, however, may be taken here as the name for a religious and moral tradition ; and in this sense it affects men who live under different governments. By contrast with Catholicism it is not highly organised; but it is able to affect, by the intense feelings of its adherents, organisations of a political and economic character. For example, probably through pressure from Jews elsewhere, the Jews of Poland and other East European countries have been

[1] The Catholic Church was in alliance with the imperialism of the old Austrian Court and against the national aspirations of the Czechs.

[2] The interest of British Protestants was based upon a neglect of differences within Christianity which appear to them important in dealing with the Vatican ; but these differences are not unknown to non-Christians.

It is related that a cock miraculously crowed in a missionary's garden in Teheran, saying in a human voice that Christianity was the true religion. A consultation of wise men was held in order to decide what should be done as a result of this message from heaven : but the wise men decided unanimously to do nothing until he cock crowed again to say which particular form of Christianity as meant.

DIFFERENCES OF CULTURE

given, under international guarantee, privileges not granted to any other religious minority.[1] Palestine, in which Jews are a minority, has been given over to Jewish control on historical grounds, which are unusual as a basis for international action. There are obviously powerful Jews in the financial and commercial circles of all the great cities of Europe and the United States; and these men tend to obscure the much more valuable qualities of Jewish scholars, poets and artists; but the religion as a whole gains power through all its adherents.

There is a surviving hostility between Judaism and Christianity with which may be connected a peculiar quasi-religious movement known as anti-Semitism. It is of importance for international politics because of the persecution of the Jews in Eastern countries. In France, Germany and Austria, Roman Catholicism is connected with mediæval customs in the hatred of Jews: but it is in Russia, Poland and Hungary that the hatred has the most startling effects. Pogroms give rise to international problems, whether security or redress is desired or emigration is promoted in order to save the remaining Jews: and pogroms with a varied slaughter of Jews have marked the first year of peace after the German armistice. The end is not yet.[2]

Islam or Mohammedanism is a third great religion with international influences. The yearly pilgrimage to Mecca from all Mohammedan lands is the concern of diplomats and officials, for it binds together the most diverse races and is a means of spreading opinion and policy in all the lands of Islam. There are divisions in Islam. The Shiah faith dominates Persia and the Sunni is more usual elsewhere. There are disagreements about the Kalifate: but popularly the world is still divided into lands of Islam and " lands of war "; and a Jihad or holy war may at any moment be advocated by enthusiasts or used by cynics.

Again, Islam may affect the international situation because great numbers of Mohammedans are under British rule and, therefore, the British Government may be specially

[1] An example of this is the agreement in the Polish Treaty that elections should not be held on a Sabbath. " Poland declares her intention to refrain from ordering or permitting elections to be held on a Saturday " (Art. II). Cmd. 223 (1919), Treaty Series No. 8.

[2] Details of anti-Jewish pogroms in Ukraine in *Manchester Guardian*, January 10, 1920; *Times*, August 5, 1919; and in Poland, *Humanité*, July 14, 1919.

careful not to offend Mohammedan feelings.[1] It is said that in parts of Africa the British favour Islam in preference to Christianity; and in Asia Minor the situation often results in the maintenance of Islam by Great Britain in rivalry with the maintenance of Christianity by France. The sentiments of Mohammedans in British India are not confined by frontiers: for example, collections of funds for Turkey were made in India in 1877 when Russia invaded Turkey; meetings of protest were held in India when Italy attacked Tripoli; there was strong feeling against Russia because of her advance in Persia in 1907; and protests have been made by Indian Moslems against the suggested dismemberment of Turkey in 1919. France also is coming to be aware of its position as a Mohammedan power in Morocco, Central Africa and possibly Syria, and this may affect French foreign policy, more especially as a powerful group in France has long been financially connected with Turkey.

Further, all races and nations which are Mohammedan have something in common which is more than a theology. Islam is a rule of life and Mohammedan Law is a political fact. It is, therefore, always possible that Mohammedans may unite in opposing other political systems; and there have been frequent fears of a Pan-Islam movement which might result in a Holy War against Europeans. This movement which began about 1850 was at first largely literary, but it was used by the Sultan of Turkey and by the Young Turks to promote a political programme for all Moslems. During the Tripoli War, Moslem societies from all parts of the world sent subscriptions to assist the Turkish Government against the Italians: and it must be remembered that not only the theology of Islam but also Moslem political ideas are dominant in parts of India, Persia, Turkey and Asia Minor, Arabia and in the whole of the population of Africa north of fifteen degrees of north latitude. This it is which makes the pilgrimage to Mecca an international fact of great importance.[3]

[1] cf. *Round Table*, January, 1920.
[2] cf. Hanotaux, *Etudes dipl.* " l'Islam français."
[3] " Present on the pilgrimage are Turks, Anatolians, Bedouin, Indians, Persians, Chinese, Javanese, Japanese, Malayans, a dozen different African races, Egyptians, Afghans, Baluchies, Swahilis and Arabs of every description. Representatives of half the races of the globe may be picked out in the mosque (at Medina) any day during the month before the pilgrimage," p. 92, " A Modern Pilgrim in Mecca," A. J. B. Wavell, ed. 1918.

DIFFERENCES OF CULTURE

Ancient history too may have its effects. It is not forgotten by scholars—and the scholars are more powerful in Islam than under Christianity—that Islam once formed the basis for supreme government in the Near East, the whole of north Africa and Spain : but recently one Moslem state after another has been overcome, over-run or dismembered. Morocco, Persia and Egypt were once independent and powerful Moslem states. Turkey, the only Moslem state treated as almost an equal of other states in 1870, has been beaten in the Tripoli War (1911), the Balkan Wars (1912, 1913) and the recent Great War. Naturally, therefore, the adherents of Islam are alarmed; and in this case, by contrast to the fear among Catholics in 1870 for the loss of the temporal power of the Pope, the diminution of the Kalifate's power and the subordination of the Koran to the law of infidels appear as racial not less than religious problems.[1]

These are but a few examples of religious problems affecting international politics. There are many others of various kinds. The government of the races of Africa involves religious problems—the position of chiefs, the laws of "taboo" and so on: the status of missionaries, both in regard to natives and in regard to the supreme government of a district, gives rise to other problems: and religion among civilised races still remains as a cover for economic purposes, an excuse for political schemes or a justification for arbitrary distinctions between one nation or party and another. Here again the situation calls for action from an international point of view, although all action seems now to be based upon the conflicting foreign policies of rival governments or parties.

Emigration.—A third group of cultural problems is to be found in the contact between peoples differing in social tradition or economic development. The best example of this is the result of the movements of workers across the frontiers of states. Emigration is one of the most important international problems, not so much because of diplomatic difficulties as because of its effects upon the emigrants themselves and upon the other workers in the country which they enter. Three kinds of emigration may be distinguished—permanent, seasonal and temporary. In permanent emigration the emigrant settles in his new country and often is naturalised there. Whole families

[1] For the problem of the Kalifate see Margoliouth in *New Europe*, April 8, 1920.

or even larger groups move in this permanent emigration; and of course it is the oldest kind of emigration known. The modern features in it are that (1) the permanent emigrant often sends money back to his home country and often also pays the fare for relatives and friends to emigrate: secondly (2) the permanent emigrant sometimes preys upon later comers, either hiring them as cheap labour or taking advantage of their ignorance and impoverishment when they first enter their new country.

Seasonal emigration is the movement across frontiers at the harvests, comparable to the movement of London labour into the Kentish hop fields. Great numbers before the war used to come from Poland into Germany and from Belgium into France, for the harvests. Italians used also to come into France for the gathering of the grapes: but by far the most interesting seasonal movement was that from Italy to the Argentine. About 50,000 Italians used to go out to the Argentine for the harvests there, and some stayed from October till April, returning for agricultural work in Italy and thus obtaining two harvest seasons in the year, one north and one south of the equator.[1] Such seasonal migration involves that great numbers of workers are not citizens or subjects of the country in which they work for a time. Questions of legal status and of insurance and other benefits, therefore, arise: for emigration in this case means not a settlement in new countries but a greater mobility of workers which will naturally increase as transport facilities improve.

A third kind of emigration, which may be called temporary, is a comparatively recent practice. It involves that the emigrant resides for three or four years in a new country and then returns with some money to his home country. Many Italians followed this practice in emigrating to the United States before the war. The results of this temporary emigration are peculiar; since (1) the emigrant is generally a man, who in his new country is without wife, child or home; (2) he does not become a citizen in his new country and has no interest in it except for what he can take out of it; and (3) he often leaves dependents in his home country insufficiently provided for. In addition to the diverse international problems

---

[1] *cf.* Bulletin No. 3, Sept., 1912, Assoc. Internat. pour la lutte contre le chômage; and also Valentini-Persini, "Protezione e legislazione di lavoro."

DIFFERENCES OF CULTURE

arising out of these different kinds of emigration, there are problems common to all movement of workers across frontiers—emigrant routes and ships, epidemic disease, emigration agencies and banks. The review and solution of these problems obviously call for the international mind to displace a mere conflict of national policies.

The extent of emigration cannot be calculated in very exact figures, for most of the countries from which emigrants came kept very inadequate statistics; and even the best kept of the statistics of immigration, those for the United States, are exact only for recent years. The following figures however give some indication of the numbers who used to emigrate before the war.

The emigration of workers across frontiers used to take place chiefly from southern European and Russian lands, from parts of Africa and from Japan and China, to North and South America. Italy for some years before the war had increased her emigration: in 1910 there were 651,475 emigrants and 872,598 in 1913. Southern Italians went generally to North and South America and Northern Italians to other European countries, but many Italian emigrants returned to their native land. Thus although about 50,000 went to the Argentine yearly, as many returned; while in U.S.A. many Italians stayed only a few years. From European countries also many return; and from all countries between the beginning of August and the end of September 1914, about 466,503 returned to Italy.

Austria-Hungary before the war sent out emigrants to the number of 247,466 in 1912, and 309,950 in 1913. Most of them went to U.S.A.; but 24,394 in 1912, and 29,460 in 1913 went to Canada. These were of various nationalities, Czechs, Slavs, Ruthenes and the rest; and although the creation of national states may now prevent such large emigration, economic conditions will probably for some time force many to seek new homes. The same is true of the lands of the old Russian Empire, from which as many as 2,527,457 left for the U.S.A. from 1873 to 1910. Poles and Jews may still desire to emigrate; and with them may come the typhus, cholera and tuberculosis which have ravaged those lands since the war. The United Kingdom is another source of emigrants; but great numbers used to go to other parts of the British dominions. In 1913, the number of emigrants was

303,685, and it is calculated that about 250,000 emigrate in a normal year. Japan is the only source outside Europe for any large emigration. In June, 1917, there were 450,773 Japanese resident abroad, of whom about 228,000 were in the U.S.A. and about 20,000 in Australia.

Countries which receive immigrants in Europe are France and Germany. Before the war Germany depended upon a seasonal immigration of about 250,000 persons from Russian Poland: and although the ports of Germany were large outlets for emigration,[1] the number of German emigrants was small, amounting to only 18,545 in 1912, of whom 13,706 went to U.S.A. France, however, is in a much more striking position. Her need for foreign labour has been great for many years, and the war has made her need still greater. In 1911 there were in France 1,159,835 aliens, of whom there were among the working classes alone 151,421 Italian men and 52,792 Italian women. Two private societies existed for recruiting agricultural labour abroad and since 1915 an official department has worked at this: during the war there was a very extensive official recruitment of munitions labour in Greece, Asia Minor and Portugal and of agricultural and other labour in North Africa.[2]

The great receiver of immigrants has been hitherto America, North and South. The United States have received an increasing number since the middle of the nineteenth century: the number rose from 619,068 in 1902 to 1,199,566 in 1907 when following the industrial crisis of that year it fell to 691,901 in 1908. There were 718,875 in 1912, 1,197,892 in 1913 and 1,218,480 in 1914; but the numbers rapidly fell during the war. In 1915 the total was 326,700, and in 1916 it was 298,826.

The nationality and the comparative culture of the immigrants changed considerably during the war. Negroes increased from 5,660 in 1915 to 7,971 in 1917; Germans decreased from 20,729 in 1915 to 9,682 in 1917; Spaniards increased from 5,705 in 1915 to 15,019 in 1917; and English decreased from 38,662 in 1915 to 32,246 in 1917.

[1] From Bremen, in January, February and March, 1913, 46,219 emigrants sailed, and from Hamburg during the same time, 35,531.
[2] Bulletin of the French Assoc. pour la lutte contre le chômage. Even before the war the employers of the Briey district recruited 49,325 foreign workers. The seasonal emigration from Belgium, Spain and Italy for the harvests and the vintage was absolutely essential for France.

DIFFERENCES OF CULTURE

In South America the immigrants have been chiefly Spanish, Portuguese and Italian but Germans have settled in great numbers in parts of Brazil and there are many British in Argentine. Problems of a social character arise when great numbers of the inhabitants of a country are not citizens or subjects of that country. The following figures are estimates for 1919 based upon official statistics :—[1]

	Aliens in Argentine	Brazil.
From France	155,406	28,364
,, Great Britain	58,822	22,249
,, Germany	60,683	123,194
,, Italy	2,303,706	366,506
,, Spain	1,522,624	478,889

The problems arising from emigration are political, economic and cultural ; but they may be all classed together here, especially as the political and cultural problems are in this matter closely allied. Economically the chief problems are as follows : (1) the supply of labour in new countries is most rapidly increased by immigration. Thus the great steel industry and some of the textile and boot industries of the U.S.A. depended upon immigrant labour ; and the whole world gains by the development of new resources, but the new country is hindered by an influx of non-citizens who have to be assimilated. (2) The possibility of emigration tends to provide alternative employment for the unemployed in countries of " exit " or to lessen the number of those who might suffer from unemployment in populous countries. It does not follow that emigration is a cure for unemployment, because in some cases—for example, if the young and the skilled emigrate—the whole level of employment may actually be lowered by emigration. (3) The supply of foreign labour often cheapens labour and depresses the standard of life of the workers.

More important still is the cultural problem (1) of the contact between races or nationalities at different stages of development. Friction may result which may make government difficult, or the emigrant may be outside the life of his new country, victimised or degraded. Again (2) it places an immense difficulty in the way of development in a new country if great numbers of adults, untrained or trained in diverse traditions, have to be

[1] *l'Economista d'Italia*, December 4, 1919.

assimilated. On the other hand (3) unless the movement of the more energetic and adventurous is free, obstacles are placed in the way of the increasing contact of thought and ability between different nations and international life is stunted.

For these and other such reasons most governments have already taken action in regard either to emigration or immigration. The countries of emigration generally wish to promote emigration; and some social classes in the new countries wish to restrict or to regulate immigration: it is worth noting that exactly the same division of opinion was evident among the Socialists at the Socialist Congress of 1907; and therefore in this matter the Socialist parties appear to have the same policies as the "capitalist" governments of their respective countries. The Australian labour parties, for example, in control of government there, have continued the obstruction to the entry of Oriental labour into tropical Australia, a district which clearly cannot be developed by a large "white" population.[1]

Emigration is promoted generally by information offices; but in most countries these offices are either those of foreign governments or administrations or are worked for private gain in connection with shipping or banking agencies. Thus in England the self-governing Dominions promote emigration, and in Europe generally there were both offices of such countries as Argentine and Brazil and many more offices of private agents. Even governmental offices have led to difficulties through the spreading of false information in regard to the new countries. In 1910 for example the offices for Brazil in Europe were closed as a result of action by European Governments.

Obviously the whole system for promoting emigration needs investigation and perhaps regulation. But besides promoting through information some countries attempt to regulate the flow of emigrants: for example, in England the Colonial Office is the administrative department chiefly concerned and the original Emigrants Information Office came under the Colonial Office. By this means it is sought to regulate the flow so as to direct emigrants to the Colonies rather than to foreign countries. Again militarist governments put obstacles in the way of the emigration of men of military use. Again in some

[1] White, "Tropical Australia."

DIFFERENCES OF CULTURE

countries depopulation may be feared and in Spain, for example, a decree prohibits the simultaneous emigration of whole villages.

Immigration, however, is the more frequent field for government action. The mere restriction of entry for aliens generally has much increased in many countries since the war;[1] indeed it seems to be doubtful whether for some years we shall get back to the old right of entry of any person into any country of which he has not transgressed the laws. It is not simply that there are regulations which enforce conditions of entry, for in many countries obstacles are placed in the way without any discoverable regulations. These symptoms of war fever may however pass.

The chief permanent systems of restricting immigration are based upon political and cultural principles. Thus lunatics, the diseased or those who are likely to become a burden to the country are generally excluded. The regulations often, as in the case of the United States, make it obligatory for the shipping company to take back without charge any immigrant who contravenes the regulations, and this makes the private agents more careful in their recruitment of emigrants than they would otherwise be. In the year from June 30, 1910, to June 30, 1911, the number deported from the United States was 20,000.[2] As in most cases the important point is not the regulations but the administrative machine, and in the United States, Canada and Australia the administration is effective. A peculiar system of restricting immigration exists in some countries, as in Canada where the law gives large powers to the Governor-General in Council to prohibit or limit the immigration of any class; in the same way the Commonwealth Immigration Act 1901-1912 gives powers to the Governor-General: and thus it would be impossible to tell from the Acts themselves what classes are in fact excluded. By this means it is found possible to exclude persons in accordance with popular judgment without being offensive to the nations of which those persons are members.

The International Labour Conference (November 1919)

[1] e.g. In Great Britain during the war a special Committee under D.O.R.A., Order 22D, had to issue permits for any alien *employee* to enter the country. The new Aliens Act continues war measures.
[2] International Conference Report on Unemployment, p. 74.

passed a resolution which will result in the appointment of an International Commission to consider and advise action in regard to the migration of workers, and therefore presumably some action may be taken on an international scale. It still remains necessary to leave some powers to the governments of new countries in which the people have definite social standards which they desire to maintain and develop. No general international interest can override the right of a civilised people to preserve its own characteristic life ; and indeed it may be an international interest that differences of national character should be preserved. Again, there is a limit to the utility of the movement of population across frontiers : for although to-day the majority are too immovable, it would not be good if the majority were without long residence in familiar and even inherited surroundings. Further, supposing emigration to occur, obviously the regulations governing the actual transit should be of an international character ; and the giving of all relevant information is obviously a duty of an international body.

These considerations suffice to show what the international problems are which arise from the fact of emigration. The solution of these problems is not separate or special, for emigration is a part of the labour problems for which administrative machinery may have to be set up on an international scale.

Social Classes.—The situation so far described is not new, since for many years it has been recognised that nationality, religion and the contact of cultures resulting from emigration are problems of international politics. But now a cloud appears on the horizon, a new fact of importance, one which may lead to problems of the most fundamental character, disturbing the very bases of social custom. The distinction, long accepted as obvious, between social classes is now no longer accepted as desirable or inevitable. We are a long way from the more simple creeds of those who first cried "Workers of the world, unite !" although that cry may yet be used with political effect. It is not, however, possible to suppose that the workers of the world will disregard their national, racial or religious differences : they will not adopt in every land a single comprehensive policy nor establish a single world-administration. Nevertheless, in every industrial country it is beginning to be perceived that there is a definite and

DIFFERENCES OF CULTURE

characteristic "labour" outlook which is not expressed in the structure of the states nor in their diplomacy.

The new situation, therefore, with which we have to reckon in international politics is that there can be and increasingly there will be joint action or action of a similar character in many lands taken by labour organisations for controlling the foreign policy of governments. The sense of difference between the workers and the governing class may be accentuated by other differences, such as those of religion and nationality, as shown above in the case of Upper Silesia ; but a new and perhaps more international problem is beginning to show itself where foreign capital is involved in an enterprise. The workers in such an enterprise, quite apart from the sense of nationality dividing them from foreign managers, foremen or resident owners, have another ground of appeal to their fellow citizens and even to their government against the absentee shareholders and directors. For example, in the Argentine "labour troubles" have developed into opposition to "foreign" capitalists, and in such cases it is difficult to say whether the division of interests most clearly understood implies opposition to an economic system or only the old opposition to foreigners.[1] Clearly, however, the groupings of labour in all countries are facts of primary importance.

If such forces become more powerful in international politics we are likely to see (1) a demand for control of foreign investment or supervision of foreign trade on behalf of the "workers," (2) a new evaluation of what matters in foreign affairs, cheap commodities, security and stability being preferred to large dividends and risks ; it is also possible (3) that there may be a kind of *irredentism* if the workers of one country secure freedom or power which they desire to see possessed also by workers of other countries. As when a nation sees beyond its frontiers men of the same language and tradition, so the workers in one country will look across their frontiers to other workers and possibly the result may be not mere expressions of brotherhood but political and economic action.

[1] *See* below, p. 104.

CHAPTER IV
UNDEVELOPED COUNTRIES

PROBLEMS in international politics, apart from the contact between sovereign states, arise from the distinction between industrialised or highly developed states and undeveloped peoples or countries. If the surface of the habitable earth may be divided into areas like Europe and North America on the one hand, and areas on the other like tropical Africa and parts of Asia, it will be found that these latter areas give rise to some of the most important conflicts of policy between the governments of the industrialised peoples. The phrases which remind one of the problem are such as "a place in the Sun," "the white man's burden," "spheres of influence" and "imperial destiny." The realities underlying these phrases are oil-seeds, wood and wood-extracts, rubber, cheap labour and new fields for investment with quick and large returns: but policy in this matter is not wholly economic, for the peoples as well as their government are still induced to support the extension of their several national powers by a vague feeling of prestige and heightened self-importance when they can say that "we have expanded" into new territories.[1]

Each of the Great Powers has within the territories controlled by it great numbers of undeveloped peoples, who are in no sense citizens of any state, but are as truly subjects of the inhabitants of Paris or London as the old Parisians and Londoners were subjects of kings before they were citizens. The "democratic" peoples rule East Africa, India, Algeria, Libya and other countries in the best traditions of despotism; and yet not the will but only the inertia and ignorance of the European peoples affect the situation, for there is no general understanding of the

[1] Compare Seeley's "Expansion of England," with its complacency of an innocent professor, with L. Vignon's "l'Expansion de la France."

responsibilities of one people for the fate of another and a weaker people, nor have even the best administrators any very clear principles to go upon. The governing factor in the situation is not ill-will but ignorance and inexperience ; for many of the instances of what is called exploitation do not result from selfishness or the greed of sinister interests, but only from the attempt to use the resources of the world. The result is often evil chiefly because the prevailing economic methods are crude and ill-adapted to the work of development in any country.

It should not be supposed, however, that the relation between industrialised and undeveloped peoples is always or everywhere objectionable. Certain great evils, leading to international agitation against cruelty or oppression, have perhaps given to this section of international politics the character of a problem and nothing but a problem : and yet even in this case, an unprejudiced review of the situation reveals much good as well as some evils. Order and a certain peculiar but not altogether objectionable kind of liberty have increased in " undeveloped " territories since governments have taken control of them. The essential fact is that peoples at different levels of economic and political development do come into contact. Traders will go to undeveloped territories, even if governments do not.[1] Native races will be affected by foreign contacts, even if we try to keep them untouched by European industrialism ; and it is, therefore, useless to consider whether or not these races should be affected, for the only questions are how they are affected and how they should be. These questions are, however, international, and they must be answered not only from the point of view of the undeveloped peoples, since other peoples may need the resources which native races are not now able to develop or to supply.

It is obvious that where the resources are many and where they are still undeveloped there is an attraction for what is called enterprise. The economic rewards are greater and more speedily attained than in older countries,

[1] The traditional method of " advance " has been by Chartered Companies, which originated when all trade was carried on by special privilege. The next step was to free the trade of a colony or dependency to all traders of the same nation, and finally to free trade to all nations. Government gradually took over administration from Companies, but often still uses administration in support of its own traders.

as is indicated in a comparison of the average dividends of companies working in new and old countries: but the problem is not wholly economic, for unsettled government or uncertain social conditions increase risks, as is indicated

CHART I

Dividends of Railway Companies

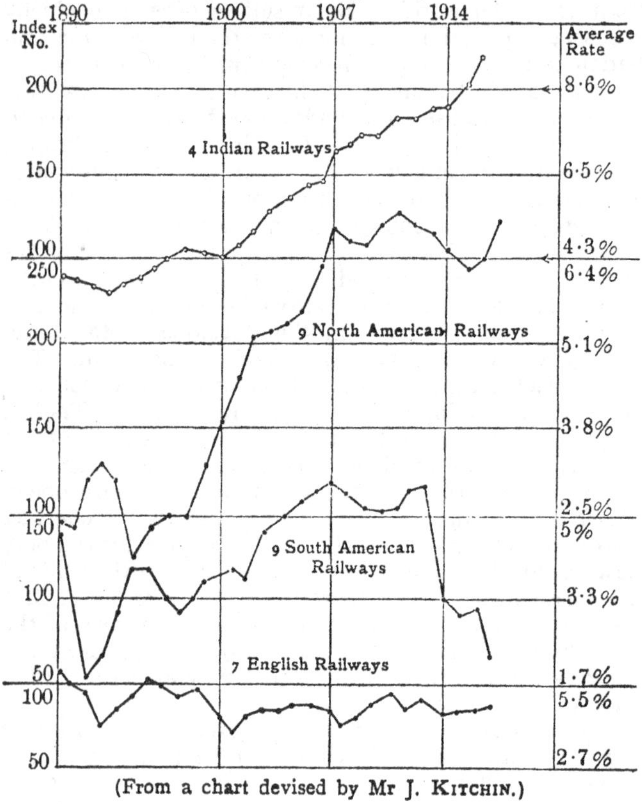

(From a chart devised by Mr J. KITCHIN.)

by a comparison of dividends of companies working in India and in South America. The comparison is made in the attached Chart between the average dividends of certain railway companies in countries of different types.[1]

[1] As an example, the Consular report for Colombia (1915, Cd. 7620-47) notes that the rate of interest for foreign private loans

UNDEVELOPED COUNTRIES

The progressive influence of the contact of industrialised and undeveloped peoples may be exemplified in the Gold Coast colony. Twenty years ago the Ashanti tribe had hardly given up its savage practices: but during the recent war, although all British troops were removed from the colony, there was no native disturbance nor even the suspicion of it; and this although in the neighbouring French colony of Dahomey there was considerable trouble. In the Gold Coast colony the cocoa exports are entirely due to production by natives on their own responsibility and for their own individual wealth. These exports have increased from 80 lbs. in 1891 to 960 tons in 1901; 35,261 tons in 1911, and 90,964 tons in 1917; and it is calculated that about £5,000,000 will be earned by the natives in the year 1919-1920. Here presumably is an instance of an increase of available commodities for the world without any resultant suffering of the producers or the native inhabitants; and the reports show how the general well-being is improving.[1]

In this case contact has developed the peoples and made the resources available of hitherto undeveloped territories. Many difficulties still remain even in regard to successful development, for, it may be asked, who gets the benefit? Or, again, do the natives share in the increasing prosperity? Or, again, in the increase of wealth is not something more valuable but more intangible lost? These questions serve to indicate the possibility of a further analysis even in regard to the best-governed dependencies: but it is necessary now to consider what happens when government is not the best. Then indeed there may be slavery, torture and murder as methods for extorting wealth for shareholders in civilised Europe and America.

An instance of what may be thought a more chequered success is to be found in French West Africa, since the reorganisation of the early years of this century. Large quantities of wood, rubber and palm-kernels are exported, but there is no indication in the official reports that the natives obtain any of the benefit, although they buy Manchester cotton goods in spite of an almost

in 1902 stood at 24 per cent., but fell to 18 per cent. in 1906, and in 1915 stood at 10 or 12 per cent. The risks were great, as wars destroyed much property from 1899 to 1902: and persons were killed to the number of 50,000 (Consular report), or 250,000 (F. X. Petre, "Republic of Colombia," p. 109, Ed. 1906).

[1] Cmd. 1-21 (1919), Colonial Office, Gold Coast.

prohibitive tariff and the attempt of French manufacturers "to imitate these goods, but without success."[1] A French writer, however, says, "The prosperity of the West African natives has improved and their capacity for buying has increased. Tempted by merchandise at low prices they have made the effort necessary to procure it for themselves, and they have developed their production."[2] The more serious fact, however, is the development of another form of "resources." A French decree of July 30th, 1919, for West Africa, extended on December 4th to Madagascar, provides for the universal compulsory service of natives for three-year periods, and 150,000 of these are to serve in Europe.[3]

In many cases tropical dependencies are usefully developed by the larger production of commodities; and skill and ability are given greater play in the building of new railways, roads or towns. Where the government is efficient and where it controls traders, the native races do not suffer more than the incidental evils of civilisation. Where, however, the government is weak, traders have freedom to take without return and the people are not even so much able to ask for return as their fellow workers in industrial cities. But worse still is the result where government becomes the agent of traders—for there the unprotected peoples have not even an hypothetical court of appeal—or the machine for enforcing a compulsory service hardly to be distinguished from slavery. There are examples enough in contemporary life, but examples from the past are perhaps less controversial.

An example of the problems of contract labour is recorded in the case of the Portuguese colonies of Angola, St. Thomé and Principé; but in referring to this record it should be understood that the records of Portuguese maladministration are, first, not unique, since other states are not blameless in their dependencies; and, secondly, the financial advantages from slavery there have accrued not to Portuguese only, but also to Englishmen and citizens of the United States.[4] In 1906 the rumours concerning

[1] Cd. 7620-33. (1915). [2] Girault, "Tariff," p. 234.
[3] Decree (secret from natives) not to be enforced if trouble results in any district! *See Journal Officiel*, December 12th, 1919.
[4] *cf.* "Portuguese Slavery," J. H. Harris, 1913. "Labour in Portuguese West Africa," 3rd Ed., 1910, W. A. Cadbury: and for really important facts see the entries in the *Statesman's Yearbook*, under Angola, etc. Note also the interesting omissions in the bibliography.

UNDEVELOPED COUNTRIES

slavery in Portuguese Africa were confirmed by reports of eye-witnesses who saw the slave-gangs, the shackles and the bodies of the murdered, and by travellers who spoke with the labourers on their way to the slavery of the cocoa plantations.[1] The slaves, or "serviçals," were captured or bought from chiefs or relatives far in the interior of Africa either by European agents or by the Bibean tribe of slave-traders. They were sold in the towns of Angola; they were "contracted" by being made to assent to a form which they did not understand, and many were taken off by steamer on a seven-days' journey to the islands of St. Thomé and Principé, which used to supply about one-fifth of all the cocoa used in the world, although their area is small. The contracts were supposed to last for about three or five years, but by threat, persuasion or fraud the slaves were generally induced to recontract. A system of repatriation has been introduced, but before about 1909 no slave who reached the islands had any hope of seeing the mainland, much less his own home again.

The conditions, of course, were not entirely due to Europeans, but arose out of native slavery and the jealousy and greed of tribes. Europeans, however, infinitely increased the evils ever since the old days of open slavery; and even the terrified natives are sometimes goaded to revolt.

The Bailandu "war" in 1902 was a kind of slave rising against the Portuguese. The slave traders ran to hiding, and the officials, with their native troops, began to shoot. In one place more than four hundred men, women and children were massacred, while the Portuguese lost only three men.[2] Revelations added to the difficulties of the Portuguese Government, and some reforms were introduced, but so few that leading cocoa manufacturers felt bound to cease importing what they regarded as slave-grown cocoa.

The position of the slaves was, in law, entirely within the domestic jurisdiction of the Portuguese Government; and, under our present primitive understanding of international politics, there would have been no ground for action by

[1] "I have been assured that each shackle represents the death of a slave, and indeed one often finds the remains of a skeleton beside a shackle. But the shackles are so numerous, that if the slaves died at that rate, even slave-trading would hardly pay." Nevinson, "A Modern Slavery," 1906, p. 113.

[2] Nevinson, *op. cit.*, p. 45.

any other state but for the fact that (1) the customers for cocoa were not all Portuguese, and (2) some of the slaves were believed to be brought from British, German and Belgian territory. The whole problem was therefore made the subject of British Foreign Office negotiations with Portugal ;[1] and official evidence did not indicate any great improvement. Thus, although frequent apologies for Portugal have been issued by British officials, usually on the amusing ground that the labourers "are now *legally* free," other officials have said " it would be useless to argue that the serviçal is not a slave merely because he is provided with a legal contract,"[2] and "their original contract was a sham and the renewed contracts were a farce."[3] The slaves are, of course, well enough fed and housed. They die by thousands of sleeping sickness, they pine for their homes and many of them prefer to die with a chance of liberty rather than live like cattle. But the suburbs of London need cocoa, and its centre needs profits, and the sources of our supplies are far away. There is no international mind at work among the people, but only a few sympathetic reformers who are regarded as cranks. And yet, even so, international action has been taken.

In 1830 Great Britain paid £300,000 to Portugal on condition that the slave trade should be forbidden. In 1842 Great Britain and the United States agreed to keep squadrons on the West Coast of Africa for the suppression of the slave trade ; in 1858 Portugal passed a law freeing all slaves in twenty years. In the Berlin Convention of 1885 fifteen states agreed to suppress the slave trade, especially in the Congo and in the interior of Africa. At the Brussels Convention of 1890 seventeen states agreed again to suppress the slave trade ;[4] and in 1913 slavery still continued.

Another example of the same kind of problem was to be found until very recently in the Belgian Congo ; but since the Belgian Government annexed the territory in 1908 reforms have been instituted. The situation under the régime of Leopold II, King of the Belgians, has, however, made a part of the existing problems of native labour in Africa, and its effects still continue. Full details

[1] Cd. 6322, Cd. 6607 (1913), Cd. 7299 (April, 1914), etc.
[2] Consul Mackie, Cd. 6322.
[3] Vice-Consul Smallbones, April 29, 1913, Cd. 7279, p. 31.
[4] Nevinson, *op. cit.*, in fine.

UNDEVELOPED COUNTRIES

can be found in official publications, and it is enough here to say that the system of using the natives was even more barbaric in the Congo than elsewhere in Africa.[1] The country was worked as a capitalist enterprise, the land, produce and the inhabitants themselves being treated as the private property of the King and about twenty of the richest families of Belgium. The Belgian people were uninformed as to the situation. The natives of a territory almost as large as Europe were slaughtered, maimed, tortured and driven into exile in order that rubber and ivory might be collected.[2] Great wealth for a few was the result, and a certain amount of gain for subordinate officials of what was in name the Congo Free State, but in fact a trading company. Abundant reasons existed for international action under the Berlin Act of 1885 and the Brussels Act of 1890, but the Governments of the world hesitated. Eventually the Belgian Government took over the administration from King Leopold, and the Congo Free State ceased to exist ; in the Charter of the new colony it is laid down that there shall be no delegation of executive authority to private persons or to companies.

The position is now regulated by a new Convention signed at St. Germain, September 10th, 1919,[3] which is in effect an amendment of the Berlin Act and the Brussels Declaration. The contracting parties " wishing to ensure by arrangement suitable to modern requirements the application of the general principles of civilisation established by the Acts of Berlin and Brussels," [4] agree that in the Congo basin and in the region thence to the Zambesi there shall be commercial equality for all nations under the Convention and freedom of navigation there and on the Niger. The various sovereign Powers " will continue to watch over the preservation of the native populations

[1] Cd. 1933 (1914) and Cd. 2097. An official circular is in Cd. 1933 (enclosure 8), p. 81, which aims at increasing the value of rubber. The policy indicated is that government was for the sake of commercial exploitation. The reform was due in part to official revelations ; but these would not have led to action unless there had been a vigorous campaign by the Congo Reform Association, founded in England in 1904, which was dissolved when its work was done in June, 1913.

[2] The area is about 909,600 sq. miles, and a population of about 15½ millons. For a recent commerical description see the address of Dr. Horn in the "Journal of the Royal Society of Arts," April 6, 1917.

[3] Cmd. 477, Treaty Series, No. 18 (1919).

[4] Preamble to the Convention.

and will in particular endeavour to secure the complete supression of slavery in all its forms and of the slave trade by land and sea."[1]

Another instance of development shows a territory in Peru, on the border of Colombia, imperfectly controlled by government and effectively exploited by commercial agents of a British Company. The Peruvian Amazon Rubber Company, Ltd., took over from June 30th, 1907, the affairs of Arava Hermanos which had recruited British negro labourers in Barbados in 1904. About 100 of these men were used in the Putumayo district as armed brigands to terrorise the native Indians, who numbered about 50,000, in and around the area exploited by the Company. The Indians were docile and divided into small family groups of about 200 each which fought one another in the forests with bows and blow-pipes. The Barbados men were themselves tortured by their masters and reduced to a state of "peonage";[2] but they and such Indians as could be forced to enslave their countrymen helped in the flogging and torturing of the population for the purpose of compelling them to bring in rubber and to do other forced labour.[3] Armed bands hunted down any Indians who tried to escape into the forests. The crimes of one of the agents, still in charge in 1910, "included innumerable murders and tortures of defenceless Indians—pouring kerosene oil on men and women and then setting fire to them; burning men at the stake; dashing the brains out of children; and again and again cutting off the arms and legs of Indians and leaving them to speedy death in their agony."[4] Pressure from the British Government induced the Peruvian Government to issue warrants against offenders but these were ineffective, and a Peruvian Commissioner was appointed in April, 1912. The Indian population had been reduced by massacre from 50,000 in 1900 to less than 10,000 in 1910 but rubber to the value of about one and a half million pounds had been put on the London market during the period. This is called the civilising of undeveloped territories.

The instances cited refer necessarily to the past; but

[1] Article 11.

[2] "Peonage" is the state of the worker who is reduced to slavery by debt to his employer.

[3] It is reported that 90 per cent. of the Indian population bore traces of flogging. Cd. 6266, p. 34.

[4] Cd. 6266, p. 36.

UNDEVELOPED COUNTRIES

it should not be imagined that torture and murder have ceased to be used as methods for earning dividends or obtaining material. Even in the territories of more powerful and more highly organised states than Peru or Portugal there is much more to be discovered ; and it is credibly reported that investigations would be useful in British North Borneo and the French Congo. This, however, will be enough to indicate what happens when the government of dependencies is not of the best. But it is well to be clear as to the origin of the evil. The cause is the method of economic development now used *in every country in the world*. That method causes great evil among the workers and resources of "civilised" and industrial countries. Pittsburg, Ancoats, St. Étienne have their own records : but the same method is more extreme in its effects on undeveloped peoples because they are less protected. It is unpractical to suggest that another economic system might be substituted for private " enterprise " with a view to profits for capital owners : but it is obvious that the first task of government should be to control the system in undeveloped countries. The interests of all nations demand this : and its practice is an obvious necessity in international politics.

Since, however, government may become the agent of that which it pretends to control, it is clear that resources of undeveloped countries might better be made available if the agent of development were neither private traders nor governments but public corporations for public service. All commodities would then be purchased from natives or residents by bodies, perhaps international in character, which existed for public service in the same sense as a gas company or a borough council providing electricity. They would be given charters to the exclusion of capitalist companies on the ground of the peculiar inappropriateness of the current economic system for operation among undeveloped peoples, and further because that system makes government difficult or contaminates its practice among such peoples.

From experience already available certain general principles can be derived, not as abstract and ideal commandments but as general statements of proved truth.

The first principle of all contact with undeveloped peoples is that administration should not be in the hands of those who are agents of commercial enterprise. This has been declared by Lord Cromer to be the principle of British rule:[1] it is embodied in the Belgian Act constituting the Congo Colony (November, 1908); and it is indeed a particular instance of the fundamental principle that government and business are two quite distinct social functions.[2] However close the relation between economic development and good government, a business enterprise aims at one kind of good and a state aims at another: and even if trade and commerce were in fact what it is claimed that they should be, public services rather than sources of private gain, government nevertheless is best when kept distinct from economic organisation.

Secondly, it is obvious that there should be efficient government in all parts of the world, so long at least as the alternative is chaos, personal caprice for a few, and suffering for many. The expansion of the territories covered by normal administration has, on the whole, been good; and although government has been too rigid in its forms and not sufficiently adaptable to new issues, the very difficulties of the contact with undeveloped peoples have compelled attempts at new methods.

Thirdly, the government of undeveloped peoples should preserve as far as possible the structure of native society while allowing that society freedom to develop on its own lines. Such a general principle, however, is by no means easy to apply. For some time the customs, language and moral traditions of undeveloped peoples or native races were suppressed, either as a conscious policy or by the accident of contact with Europeans. The French, for example, in their far Eastern colonies introduced the French language and French political and judicial systems.[3] It is now taken for granted that good administration should be based upon native law and custom, and that is obviously an advance: but what is native law and custom? The

[1] Thus Lord Cromer said (Hansard, H. of L. February 24th, 1907): " The first principle is that the duties of administration and the commercial development of the country should not be vested in the same individuals. The counter principle of associating the two functions we tried ourselves years ago with the old East India Company, and though we had at the head of it many men who were not only merchants but statesmen, the system of government, if not a failure, was at best but a very modified success." The same idea is worked out in Cromer's " Ancient and Modern Imperialism."

[2] *See* below, " Diplomacy," p. 127.

[3] *cf.* Reinsch, " Colonial Administration."

best administrators have sometimes made the mistake of supposing that the essence of native society lay in the maintenance of a crude system of tribal responsibility and the authority of chiefs: and the ludicrous result has occurred that Europeans have forced chiefs upon native tribes in the name of native customs even when the chief-system was unknown, as among the Kikuyu in East Africa ; or Europeans have established and supported as chiefs men who were the laughing-stock of the natives themselves, as the French did in the Marquesas.[1] Worse than all, by the enforcement and maintenance of obsolete or European-made " native customs " the natives are prevented from development on their own lines, while they are made subservient to the economic and political ends of the European. They are kept under chiefs when they would have developed out of such autocracy if the autocracy had not been supported by European administrators, while that autocracy has been used as means of raising labour for European needs. Thus even in well-governed dependencies the problem of labour has to be faced. Indirect pressure can be exerted either through the chiefs or by means of taxation or by other administrative means (registration, the corvée, etc.) to force the native to work for the white man, when the alternative is not mere inactivity but work in native fashion for the native's own ends and in consonance with his own moral standards. It is true that Europe needs coffee, rubber and palm-oil : it is true also that the natives may be individually more wealthy if they work for wages : but in the process the natives may be morally degraded in the pursuit of wealth or reduced to the unenviable status of a new and more helpless tropical proletariat.

The truth is that the civilised nations having made great advances in mechanism and having improved or more fully used the resources of nature, are still incompetent enough in organising themselves and even more incompetent to organise the lives and control the future of undeveloped territories and peoples. Therefore, although the solution of the problems here mentioned needs great labour, there should be a very great hesitation in applying supposed solutions and a very great flexibility in the methods of administration. At this task no one nation

[1] *cf.* Stevenson's description of a French-made chief in his " South Seas."

can succeed alone; the problem and its solution must obviously be regarded as international.

The situation so far described has been chiefly due to the development of undeveloped territories, and the treatment of native labour within the acknowledged territory of a fully developed state. These problems may appear to be domestic rather than international; but they become international because (1) the products of one state's tropical dependencies may be used in the industries of another state, as in the case of cocoa from St. Thomé, used by British and German firms, or (2) the action taken in one state's dependencies may make government difficult in the neighbouring dependencies of another state, as in the case when bad administration in parts of the Congo basin causes native unrest in other parts of Africa.

Again, there is a very ancient tradition that colonies and dependencies are "possessions" or estates to be used for the special benefit of the people whose administration controls them. Hence arises the international problem connected with the phrase the Open Door, which indicates a policy under which no preference is given to the traders of the controlling nation. The situation in most dependencies of most countries at present is the reverse of the open door; there are tariffs and other special means by which the trade of the governing country is secured in its dependencies against competition with foreign trade; but international policy in regard to such areas as the Congo and Morocco has been able to secure the open door there, and special provisions of the same kind relate to parts of China. Great Britain, Holland and Germany before the war left trade largely free. France, on the contrary, has hitherto pursued a policy of exclusion, and the United States has adopted the same policy in its own dependencies. Under the French Government there are now three kinds of régime in dependencies: (a) assimilated tariffs (i.e. similar to those of France) in Algiers, West Indies, etc.; (b) a special régime (tariff "personality") in West Africa, Oceania, St. Pierre and Miquelon; and (c) the open door in Morocco, Ivory Coast, etc.[1] The Berlin Act of 1885 secured the Open Door in the Congo Basin; an agreement of 1898 between Great Britain and France opened one million square miles of

[1] Girault, "Colonial Tariff Policy of France." *cf.* Culbertson, "Commercial Policy."

Africa and the Algeceiras Convention of 1906 opened Morocco. But governments still use dependencies as estates, and rivalries therefore occur.

Similar circumstances arise when the undeveloped territory is outside the acknowledged territory of an industrialised people or a powerful state. The foreign territories in which the more highly organised states seek special advantages are all to be found in Asia and Africa, although parts of European Russia may since the war have become "spheres of influence" for some states—that indeed cannot be ascertained until some years have run and the lands of the old Russia are more settled. The principles involved, however, are the same wherever a highly-organised state or people take control over an "undeveloped" territory. Such territory may be regarded as part of another sovereign state as in the case of China and Persia; or it may be without any state-control before the highly organised state takes control, as in the case of the Sudan, Rhodesia and parts of the Sahara. Intermediate between these two classes of territory are the colonies or outlying districts of weak states as Tripoli was before the Italo-Turkish war, or as parts of South America still are.

The existence of these undeveloped territories is a source of friction between peoples largely because there is no international principle or policy for increasing the use of the undeveloped resources of the world.[1] Clearly it is an advantage that more rubber, wood or minerals should be available for use; clearly also such commodities in some territories would not be put on the market by their native inhabitants. Further, the growth of industrial enterprise causes the search for new sources of supply and new fields for investment; and apart from economic motives, the states of the world are interested that the whole of the habitable earth shall be brought under effective government. On the other hand, the legitimate desire for goods is not usually supposed to justify a seizure of other people's goods; the need for minerals is not morally supposed to justify dispossession of the users of the surface still less their enslavement for obtaining the minerals for others; and finally there may

[1] *See* W. Lippman: "The Stakes of Diplomacy." The scramble for gain should be transformed to a mutual agreement for each to serve all.

be considerable doubt as to what is the true development of a territory or a people, and the people themselves may perhaps be supposed to judge for themselves. Again, the traders of different nationality are usually rivals. Each national group seeks resources for its own industries, or a sphere for its own investment, and the several governments, perhaps not unwillingly, are drawn into the contest. Such are the problems which arise from the existence of undeveloped territories and the contact between highly-organised states and undeveloped peoples. It need hardly be said that it is no solution of these problems to suggest that what is undeveloped should be left to be so; for, first, if the states hold back, the traders will not; and the contact between traders and undeveloped peoples is even worse than the contact between such peoples and the officials of states; secondly, the world really needs more goods, and some method must be discovered of utilising untouched resources.

The general situation, however, can be understood best by reference to examples. China is in theory a sovereign state; it is indeed a republic, an ancient civilisation, an industrious and numerous people, and a vast source of material wealth, both as a market and as productive.[1] Although the native peoples are highly organised, the government is more "international" than in any other country; for in government employ in 1917 there were 1,105 British, 1,003 French, 533 German, 463 Russians, 207 Japanese, 174 Americans, 75 Italians, 191 Belgians, 59 Austrians and 158 of other foreign nations.

More significant, however, than the number of foreign officials is the extent and character of the foreign control of finance and transport.[2] Before 1908 the Chinese Government raised loans from separate national groups generally on the condition of putting foreigners in control of the enterprise for which the money was needed. The capital of the South Manchurian Railway Syndicate is almost entirely supplied by the Japanese Government; and it controls 680 miles of railway, and also works mines, coalfields and steamships. So also in the Yusman province the French Government of Indo-China backs a

[1] The Republic was established in 1912. In 1915 the President attempted to establish a monarchy with himself as head of a new dynasty. Revolt followed and the President died on June 6, 1916, and a new President kept the Republic.

[2] "Modern China," by Sih-Gung Che'ng, August, 1919, p. 208 *seq*.

railway syndicate with 288 miles of railway on Chinese soil. The management is foreign and the concessions were granted under pressure from foreign governments. The unsuccessful war of 1894 drove China to borrow, and one loan was arranged with a Franco-Russian group, two with an Anglo-German group. Since 1908 the foreign groups instead of competing have united to control the money market for China, and the control was internationalised in the Five Power loan of 1913. The policy declared by the British foreign office was the " internationalisation of all future loans."[1] The loan was granted on a mortgage of the Salt Gabelle, which had to be organised by foreigners with a British Chief Inspector. Therefore, although the Chinese Government is not yet in the position of Egypt under the International Financial Commission, her sovereignty is metaphorical, and she is in fact treated by foreign governments as an " undeveloped country."

The foreign debt of China in 1916 was £171,906,000, of which about £44,780,000 was owed to British, £31,000,000 to Germans, £12,000,000 to Japanese, and about £7,000,000 to the United States. The debts are secured on the Chinese revenues and foreigners manage and collect these revenues.

The Japanese took Formosa after the war with China (1895), but were prevented from taking parts of the mainland by Russia and France. In 1897 the Germans seized Kiau-Chau, and next year obtained a lease for it. Russia in 1898 took Port Arthur and its district on lease, and in 1900 she occupied Manchuria. The Russo-Japanese war ended in 1905 with the transfer of part of Manchuria and of Port Arthur to Japan. Great Britain meanwhile in 1898 took a lease of Wei-Hai-Wei and some mainland territory facing Hong Kong. In the same year France took a lease of the Bay of Kuang-Chau-Wan, and in 1899 she took possession of two islands there. The leases are as metaphorical as the sovereignty of China; but the position has been considerably modified by the war. Russia and Germany are no longer competitors in the attempt to secure spheres of influence; and during the war France and Great Britain were entirely absorbed in war efforts. The field has therefore been left open to Japan, who improved her opportunities during the war, first by a treaty with the old Russia which gave her partial freedom,

[1] Cd. 6446, quoted in Che'ng.

and also probably by entering into negotiations with Germany.[1] While Europe was otherwise engaged, the Japanese lent money to China and Japanese investments increased there. Citizens of the United States, however, have also increased their commercial connections with China.

By the Peace Treaty with Germany the Shantung province was placed under a partial Japanese predominance, and this excited a serious anti-Japanese movement among the students in China, beginning on May 4th, 1919.[2] A boycott of Japanese goods was partly successful and the militarist government of the Chinese Republic was apparently moved to make concessions to the students only by a fear that the army itself was being " corrupted."

It is recognised that the Japanese support militarism in China and that the present government is militaristic: it is also recognised that the Chinese tradition is democratic and not autocratic as the Japanese. But these are passing phases. The more important facts for the present purpose are the signs of the intervention of foreign capital and possible divisions of spheres. A new bank has recently been set up in Pekin with a capital of two million pounds, half paid-up: the president is a late Prime Minister of China and the vice-president is a late director of the British American Tobacco Company. It is believed that American money will be lent on the security of the wine and tobacco monopolies " which will be reorganised by an American associate Inspector General with powers equivalent to those of the British Inspector General of the Salt Gabelle."[3] Meantime Vickers, which has already strong connections in Japan, secured an order from the Chinese Government for aeroplanes, for which a loan of £1,800,000 at 8% is to be raised. " Vickers are not only supplying the aeroplanes but

[1] The Japanese envoy, Ota, at Stockholm in March, 1916, was concerned in unexplained business.

[2] The Japanese wish to believe that this anti-Japanese feeling is incited by British and Americans. See extracts from Japanese papers in the *Japan Weekly Chronicle*, May 22, 1919.

[3] *Times*, December 22. " The new agreement appears to have been made independently of the U.S.A. Government by the Pacific Development Corporation. The new Commercial and Industrial Bank of China has Chien Nung-Hsua as President, Mr. J. A. Thomas as Vice-President, and includes among its shareholders President Hsu-Shih-Chang, ex-Presidents Li Yuang-hung and Fengkuo-chang as well as Chang-Ssun."

UNDEVELOPED COUNTRIES

are also sending out experienced pilots to train Chinese pilots."[1]

Mexico is another instance of the peculiar relation of industrialised peoples to undeveloped territories. During the rule of President Porfirio Diaz (1876–1911) the Mexican Government was able to guarantee the rights of all holders of property, and it is calculated that at least 200 million pounds of British and 300 million pounds of United States money was invested in Mexico. Since 1911 there has been a succession of Presidents,[2] continual warfare, confusion, disease and no settled government. Naturally the mines, oilfields, railways and banks suffered greatly. The revenues, for example, of the National Railways of Mexico, a joint British and U.S.A. Company, which used to be about £7,000,000 had dropped in 1919 to about £5,000.[3] In December 1913 the company had announced that it was unable to pay interest due on January 1, 1914, in cash.[4] The Mexicans who happened at any moment to control most force were able to tax, confiscate and otherwise harass foreign owners : and in consequence an agreement was reached by Great Britain and the United States that neither would give " diplomatic support " to any of their respective citizens claiming rights acquired since January 1, 1913.[5] Meantime the holders of shares are in a peculiar position. The Mexican Cotton Estates Co. (British) was unable in 1913 to realise its cotton crop, valued at £300,000. The Mexican Government acquired control of the Mexican National Packing Co. (U.S.A.) in April 1914 : and no interest has been paid on mortgage bonds. The great oil companies are, however, perhaps the most important politically; for example the Mexican Eagle Oil Co., which acquired the concessions of S. Pearson & Son, is connected with the Eagle Oil Transport Co., and is now controlled by the Shell-Royal Dutch Combine. The Mexican Petroleum Co. (U.S.A.) has

---

[1] *Times*, October 13, 1919.

[2] Madero, 1911 ; Huerta, 1913 ; Lascurian, Garza, Chazaro, Carranza, 1915.

[3] H. G. Richards, British Vice-Consul, in *Daily News*, September 5, 1919.

[4] *Stock Exchange Year Book*, 1919, p. 387. Similar difficulties were met by the other British railway companies, the Mexican Eastern, the Mexican Railway, the Mexican Southern, the Mexico North-Western, and the Michoacan and Pacific.

[5] Cd. 7463, Oil Properties and Mining Rights in Mexico.

600,000 acres of oil-bearing properties in Mexico and is connected with the American group of oil companies. There were, in 1914, 55 American companies, 21 Mexican companies and 13 British companies for operating in Mexico, and the capital involved is said to have been £19,500,000 American, £15,000,000 British and £500,000 Mexican.[1] Since the loss of security for property powerful groups have been formed, in Great Britain an international committee of twenty bankers and in the U.S.A a National Association for the Protection of American Rights in Mexico.[2] These groups inevitably influence the policies of their governments, as will be explained in chapter V.: and the process of adjustment in the international situation of Mexico is still developing.

In the case of some countries the advent of persons or authorities bent on developing their resources has cost the inhabitants their political independence. One such country is Korea. The Japanese in 1894 fought against China, under whose rule Korea then nominally was. The Japanese Government announced to the world then and often afterwards that it stood for the independence of Korea.[3] The Japanese also announced that no change would be made in the relation of Korea to foreign nations.[4] The Russo-Japanese War left Japan supreme in Korea. The country was occupied by Japan: and although in 1908 the Japanese Resident declared that Japan would not annex Korea, in 1910 an announcement was made that it was annexed. The Emperor was made into a " king " and kept under surveillance, and a Colonial Company, of which the dividends were guaranteed by the Japanese Government, bought up land on which Japanese were installed. It is said that the incoming Japanese practised the arts of the money-lender rather than those of the farmer.

[1] *Statesman's Year Book*, 1914, p. 1,083.

[2] *Times*, " City Notes," January 8, 1920. " The question of financial assistance to Mexico is largely bound up with politics. . . . The interests of foreign capitalists in Mexico are in the hands of a strong banking committee representative of British, French and American bond and stock holders."

[3] Japan bound itself by treaty with Korea (August 26, 1894) to maintain the independence of Korea. By treaty with Russia (1898) and Great Britain (1902) the same pledge was given.

[4] By treaty (August 12, 1906) with Great Britain, Japan is recognised to have " paramount interests in Korea," and in November 1905, Korea, by treaty, gave over her foreign affairs to Japanese control.

UNDEVELOPED COUNTRIES

In March 1919 the king died and his funeral was the occasion of demonstrations by the Koreans at which the cry for independence was raised. The people in general appear to have been strongly moved and crowds gathered, which although unarmed, created some alarm among the Japanese authorities. Japanese soldiers shot into the crowds and the official Japanese account says that there were 399 killed : arrests were made and torture by whipping as well as imprisonment appears to have overawed the people. Order was restored within a month.

The enterprise here shown appears to have been largely governmental, although Japanese capital has now considerable interests in Korea. It is not clear however whether any principle other than " order " is alleged by the government as the basis for their action. When criticism is made of the position of Japan in Korea, the patriotic Japanese refers to the position of England in Egypt or of the United States in the Philippines : and indeed the principles involved do not appear to differ, although the methods used are less crude in some such cases.

Turkey granted a semi-independence to Egypt in a treaty with Great Britain, Prussia and Russia of 1840. Further independence was granted to Egypt by its suzerain Turkey in 1867. In 1875 the Egyptian Government was unable to meet its creditors and a joint control of France and Great Britain was initiated. In 1877 Egypt sent men officially to the Turkish army to fight against Russia, and in 1879 the Sultan dismissed the Khedive, after which France and England controlled Egypt jointly until in 1882 Great Britain was left to suppress the rebellion of Arabi Pasha and the country was occupied.

In 1888 the Suez Canal Treaty preserved the suzerainty of Turkey over Egypt and a yearly tribute was paid. In 1904 in the Declaration as to Morocco and Egypt the British Government expressly declared that it had " no intentions of altering the political status of Egypt " : and this is parallel to the second Article of the same Declaration in which the French Government declared that " they had no intention of altering the political status of Morocco." [1] In 1897 Greek consuls left Egypt on the outbreak of the war between Greece and Turkey, thus implying that Egypt was Turkish territory ; but in 1911

[1] *See* below, p. 130.

Italian consuls did not leave Egypt during the Tripoli War, which may have implied that the position had changed. Turkey in fact seems to have accepted Egypt as a sort of British protectorate even then: and on December 17, 1914, Egypt was formally declared by the British Government to be a protectorate. The problem, however, is not solved.

China, Korea, and Egypt are or were states; but the same external effort to control resources may be found in the case of dependencies of weak states.

An ultimatum was presented by Italy on September 26, 1911, informing Turkey that " the state of disorder and neglect in which Tripoli and Cyrenaica are left by Turkey " was a grievance and that a change was necessary for Italy as a " vital interest by reason of the small distance of those countries from the coasts of Italy." Twenty-four hours were given to the Turks to order that no opposition should be offered to Italian military invasion. A reply was given by Turkey at 6 a.m. on September 29 in the most abject terms; but at 10 a.m. on that day the Italian Embassy at Constantinople presented a note to Turkey saying that as " no satisfactory reply had been received," war was declared.[1] Thus about five days had elapsed since the world was aware that Italy had any such grievance against Turkey as might lead to war; and in regard to the non-development of Tripolitana, unkind critics pointed out that Sardinia, Sicily and Southern Italy were not usually supposed to be well " developed." At the end of October the Italian Government announced that Tripolitana and Cyrenaica were " placed under the full and complete sovereignty of the Kingdom of Italy." The Italian Government had violated the Hague Convention as to the settlement of disputes, the Treaty of Paris of 1856 and that of Berlin of 1878, as regards the integrity of the Turkish Empire. In " annexing " territory without a treaty it had violated a fundamental principle never hitherto violated except by the British in 1900 in the Transvaal: and in the case of the Transvaal the suzerainty of Great Britain was at least a possible hypothesis.

[1] *cf.* " Come siamo andati in Libia," Florence, 1914. It is there stated that in April 1911, the officers of the Italian army were supplied with manuals of Arabic-Italian conversation, p. xviii. *See* also Sir Thomas Barclay, " The Turco-Italian War."

UNDEVELOPED COUNTRIES

In 1901 France and Italy entered into some agreement in which Tripolitana and Cyrenaica were treated as Italy's "sphere of influence." The only bank at Tripoli was a branch of the Banco di Roma, through which Italian money was invested in enterprises in the district.[1] The Italian Government subsidised the only line of steamers doing coastal services there. It also subsidised schools with about 900 pupils and even in the few schools subsidised by France the Italian language was taught.[2] Thus Italy was concerned with the partial development of the district. There was a sudden rumour, however, in 1911 that another power, Germany, might obtain from Turkey a loan of an African port and it is believed that this led to the sudden action by the Italian Government: but that is ancient history.

It is more important to notice that under Italy the district may become not only a reserve of Italian trade, although under Turkey all trade had equal chances, but that Italy may also push on to influences in the hinterland, where the Senussi hold the oases,[3] and the spheres of British and French influence are ill-defined. Beyond the desert lies the rich tropical source of raw material for industries and across the desert are the caravan routes.[4]

A new move took place during the war; for when it was found necessary by the Allies to induce Italy to join them, the secret Treaty signed in London on April 26, 1915, made the following arrangement:—Article XIII. "Should France and Great Britain augment their African colonial dominions at the expense of Germany, those two Powers recognise in principle that Italy will be entitled to claim some equitable compensations, notably in the regulation in her favour of questions concerning the frontiers of the Italian colonies of Eritrea, of Somaliland and of Libya and of the neighbouring colonies of France and Great Britain." Tripolitana and Cyrenaica are now called Libya and the negotiations are said to have involved an offer at Paris by

---

[1] It has been said that Vatican money was invested in Tripoli and that this was a reason for the surprising enthusiasm shown by the Roman authorities for the Italian Government's adventure; but clearly this may be an anti-Papal suggestion.

[2] Barclay, *op. cit.*, p. 57 *sq.*

[3] *id. op. cit.*, p. 83.

[4] The myth of phosphates and sulphur in Libya was used to promote the conquest, as is proved in "Come Siamo Andati," etc., pp. 1-22.

Lord Milner of a zone to the east of Libya including the oasis of Jazabub, where the Senussi rule. The French have rectified their frontier on the other side and to the south, and a joint railway scheme now connects Tunisia and Libya.[1]

An example of another method of subordinating undeveloped countries to the existing state system is to be found in the agreement entered into by France and Great Britain in May 1916 in regard to Turkish territories (the Sykes-Picot agreement). New Arab states were to be divided into two zones in one of which France and in the other Great Britain was to have " priority in regard to enterprises and local loans," [2] as well as " exclusive right to provide advisers or foreign officials at the request of the Arab state." In addition France was to take under control a large territory south and east of the Taurus, while Great Britain was to take Mesopotamia. There was no hint of " mandates." Alexandretta in the French territory was to be a " free port in so far as concerns the commerce of the British Empire," and Haifa, in Great Britain's control, was to be a free port for the commerce of France. Italy was to come in for " a share, equal to theirs" under Article 9 of the secret Treaty of April 26, 1915, taking territory north and west of the Taurus as far as Smyrna, which was to be a free port for France and Great Britain as Italy was to have similar privileges at Alexandretta and Haifa. in accordance with a later agreement. These are, of course, war measures and the plans then made may not be realised : but the example is enough to show how the more powerful states arrange for the disposition of spheres of influence and with what commercial objects. Such are the relations of industrialised peoples under their governments to undeveloped or at least non-industrial peoples and territories.

The situation is still uncontrolled by any governing political principles. It has been found, as in the case of China, that international agreement and joint action is better in some ways than rivalries of national groups in the search for concessions : but in some cases, as in Persia and perhaps in Abyssinia, it appears that an informal

---

[1] *Times*, January 6 and January 7, 1920.

[2] The words quoted are those of the agreement. The text was published in the *Manchester Guardian*, January 8, 1920, and relevant documents in the same paper for January 10, 1920.

UNDEVELOPED COUNTRIES

international agreement leaves a particular territory as a sphere for the nationals of one state.[1] Again, it seems to be agreed that conditions may be laid down by other governments if any state is granted predominant interest in any sphere; but the whole subject is full of obscurity, for in general the practice of governments is empirical and not based upon any clearly conceived principles. It is an example of the small amount of political thought and imagination so far devoted to international affairs: for obviously all peoples stand to gain by the development of the resources of the world, its minerals, its trees and foodstuffs, its harbours and trade routes, and yet there is no accepted policy still less any organisation for this common task.

---

[1] L. S. Woolf, "Empire and Commerce in Africa," gives full details as to Abyssinia as well as further typical instances of economic Imperialism, the policy of governments obsessed with trade or pushed by traders.

CHAPTER V

INTERNATIONAL TRADE

(a) *Governmental action*

THE economic interests of men concern the production and distribution of goods, and all that is usually connected with wealth. These interests may, therefore, be distinguished from the political interest, order and liberty, or justice; and in fact there are two quite distinct groups of men in all countries, "business" men, dealing with production and distribution, and "political" men, either statesmen directing policy, or civil servants or soldiers or sailors, carrying it out. The connection between business and political men and between individuals in the two groups is very important for international politics. For example, the financier will give a dinner at which a Foreign Minister may hear of certain investments being placed in an undeveloped country. It is important for the Foreign Minister to know what interests are represented; and, on the other hand, the financier may receive information as to possible political troubles. The two groups are naturally connected for the sake of information valuable to each. But the connection is sometimes closer. The Minister or Secretary may have power to grant trading privileges, and the financier may have power to give or withhold on certain conditions the financial facilities for developing the country in question. Arrangements are therefore made and understandings entered into between the economic and the political groups. It is not implied that this is necessarily sinister or dangerous. The world's products are increased by such measures, and government is often made easier where the financial powers are not opposed to the administration. But obviously there may be opportunities for privilege, to the detriment of the general public; and there may be vast proceeds for individuals earned by objectionable methods, as is evident from the examples already quoted in regard to undeveloped countries.

Traders naturally take advantage of any new situation out of which they may derive profit.[1] They are willing to use political passions in order to extend their trade at the expense of their rivals, as when the British manufacturer urges customers to buy British goods, meaning only his goods; and sometimes without any deliberate trade policy, new wealth accrues to traders because of political complications. For example, when the Great War broke out, the Germans had to cease buying palm kernels in West Africa. The prices dropped, and as their competitors were helpless, the British merchants formed a combine which kept down the price paid to the natives and put up the price charged to the users.

The advantage of pushing trade, however, is not all on the side of the traders, for politicians with an eye to " prestige " or with a policy of expansion may achieve their purpose by making connections with trading interests; and it is often difficult, when government interests are interwoven with those of a trading company, to say whether the politicians are using the financiers or the financiers the politicians. In either case, however, probably the controlling group has no very clear principles as to method, and only a very simple view of the purposes of policy. For example, the British Government gains by holding shares in the Suez Canal Company, and protection of the route to India was probably just as much a reason for the British position in Egypt as any desire of bondholders to secure their bonds. A more recent example of the partnership of government and trade is in the Anglo-Persian Oil Company, of which the British Government holds two-thirds of the £3,000,000 ordinary capital, the other third being held by the Burmah Oil Company. The British Government has also subscribed to its share of

---

[1] It is known, for example, that a box entering Palestine during Allenby's advance, supposed to contain Red Cross supplies, really contained pumping machinery for the Standard Oil agents. The *Temps* of March 2, 1920, contains an illuminating article, saying that if Kurdistan is to be a new state, France must control its oil and minerals. " Si le gouvernement français ne vent pas que l'exploitation de ces richesses échappe tout à fait à notre pays appauvri pas la guerre, on ne pent vraiment pas lui en faire un reproche." It is all for the sake of the widows and orphans impoverished by the war.

the new issue of December 1919. There may be some guiding conception for policy in regard to the need of oil for warships, as appears from the discussions in 1914,[1] but it is to be noted that the financial interests of the British Government complicate its relations to the Persian Government. The expansion of the company followed the signing of the Anglo-Persian agreement of 1919,[2] and the Persian Government is held to be in debt to the Company because of the cutting of a pipe line in 1915. The chairman was of opinion in December 1919, that " a great Company like this flies the British flag and upholds British interests in many parts of the world and is contributing in no small measure to cement friendship with Persia, to which we know in the highest political quarters great importance is attached."[3] It is interesting also that the British Government in this instance is Lord Inchcape, who represents the Government on the Board and is also chairman of the P. and O. Company.[4] A new Syndicate for Railways in Persia unites the Anglo-Persian Company with the Persian and Mesopotamian Corporation (of which Lord Inchcape is chairman), Armstrongs, Vickers, Ellermans, the Imperial Bank of Persia, etc., and thus secures British interests in those parts.[5]

The same method of sharing in a financial enterprise has been used for political ends, for example, by the Japanese Government, which owns most of the shares in the South Manchuria railway syndicate.[6] The syndicate now controls 680 miles of railway, exploits mines and coalfields, maintains a steamer service, and supplies gas and electricity to towns in Manchuria. It is an instance, then,

[1] Hansard, H.C., June 17, 1914. Labour supported the scheme. *cf.* Cd. 7419, for particulars of the scheme.

[2] Cmd. 300 (1919), Agreement of August 9th, 1919. Great Britain to supply " advisers," munitions of modern type and a loan of £2,000,000 at 7 per cent. secured on the Customs.

[3] Speech at General Meeting, by Sir C. Greenway, chairman, London, December 8, 1919. Further commitments of the Persian Government to the British Imperial Bank are given below, p.   .

[4] Details were given by Mr. Chamberlain in the Commons, Hansard, Commons, December 3, 1919. The British Government, disguised as the Anglo-Persian Oil Company has a fleet of oil-tankers, a refinery at Swansea, controlling interests in the Scottish Shale Oil companies and some distributing concerns, but these are outside the purview of international politics.

[5] *Times*, " City Notes," February 18, 1920.

[6] Cheng, " China," p. 209. Of the subscribed capital of 120 million yen, the Japanese Government holds 100 million.

INTERNATIONAL TRADE

of a government entering into trade for political purposes in a foreign country, and similar examples may be found in the case of nearly every strong government in the industrialised states.

The weaker governments of the world often make their own arrangements with financial groups, and the problems resulting from these relationships tend to become international and to involve the governments of those countries whose financial groups control foreign loans. The various private creditors of weak or ill-organised governments are sometimes organised as a unit for dealing with dishonesty or incompetence on the part of a foreign government. For example, the British Corporation of Foreign Bondholders[1] has been concerned in the settlement of foreign public debts amounting to about a thousand million pounds. The character of the situation in the relation of government to private creditors does not always reflect glory upon the sovereign state; for example, in 1918, " the External Debt of Honduras enters on its forty-sixth year of total default"; and "there has been some agitation in the local papers with regard to the expediency, if Honduras wishes to preserve its independence, of settling its foreign obligations."[2] Obviously, whatever defects the financial groups may have, the independence of a sovereign state may sometimes mean the opportunity for incompetent or dishonest groups in control of government. An example of the commitment of a powerful government, owing to the foreign debt of a weak state, is to be found in Liberia, to which the United States Government advanced five million dollars in 1918, following representations made at Washington by the British Corporation of Foreign Bondholders. Similar activities are undertaken on behalf of their own national groups by Councils for foreign bondholders in Paris and New York.

In some cases the foreign creditors form international groups for dealing with a weak government. The administration of the Ottoman Public Debt, for example, is completely international: and although the funds collected during the war were paid in only to German and Austrian creditors, nevertheless the international machinery

---

[1] Founded 1876: Board of Trade licence, 1873; incorporated under Act of 1898.

[2] Report of Council of the Corporation of Foreign Bondholders, 1918, p. 24.

survived and the creditors of other nations were credited with amounts actually collected and only awaiting the readjustment of exchange to be paid in. The Council of Administration of the Public Debt was constituted in 1881 and controls revenue from monopolies, duties and some taxes, as well as the issue of other loans.

Similarly in the case of Egypt joint action of French and British financiers in 1877 was followed by the appointment in 1878 by the British and French Governments of Commissioners to administer a new loan: the system being modified by the Anglo-French agreement of 1904.[1] That, however, is ancient history; and the problems of international politics in this regard are problems of the past commitments of governments and financial groups; but the process has not ceased. The same kind of situation appears to be developing in the Baltic States and in the Caucasus: foreign loans to governments still insecure may influence or be influenced by the policy of powerful states whose citizens are creditors.[2]

Governments, however, do not always act in partnership with trading enterprises; and even in international affairs governments generally affect economic issues by their own separate action. Such action depends upon the general truth that many states are economic units in some sense and most states tend to be completely separate economic units.

The classification and grouping of states suggested in

[1] cf. Brailsford, "War of Steel and Gold," for arguments against financiers, and Hartley Withers' "International Finance" for arguments against politicians. The loans were required for the expenses of the Khedive, some private, some "national." In 1856-1859 the Khedive was ordering the new steel guns from Krupp's, which made Krupp's name and also his foreign trade.

[2] cf. *Times*, "City Notes," January, 5, 1920: "Very large sums have already been advanced to the Governments of the Baltic provinces by British firms, with the object of restoring trade activity in those regions and they would extend their efforts if some form of guarantee of political stability could be obtained. These firms are eulogistic of the assistance given by the Foreign Office and the British Government representative in the Baltic provinces, but more remains to be done. Already a British firm has been appointed agent for the disposal of flax produced in the Baltic provinces. Arrangements are being made to obtain an equitable distribution of the flax, and thanks to the enterprise of the British firm referred to, the larger proportion of the flax will be reserved for British spinners." The National Metal Bank Scheme is set out in the *Manchester Guardian*, January 17, 1920.

the first chapter was based upon political organisation, but a not less important classification is that based upon the comparative amount of foreign trade carried on by the peoples of the several states. The foreign policy of a government must have regard to the amount and character of such trade and in that sense at least the state must be regarded as an economic unit. The available statistics of international trade chiefly refer to import and export across administrative frontiers; and this gives an artificial air of verisimilitude to the idea that such trade is essentially an interchange between peoples under distinct governments. This is not the place for an argument in economic theory, but even in the study of international politics it is well to be on one's guard against too simple a view of economic facts. The statistics of " foreign " trade do indeed show how closely the economic life of each people is bound up with the economic life of the world at large ; but it does not follow that the fundamental fact of world economics is an interchange between peoples under separate governments.[1] Indeed it should be equally possible and it would be much more instructive, if the statistics showed an interchange not between countries but between industries, regardless of state frontiers. International trade is an interchange of services and products between groups of producers and consumers and not an interchange between peoples organised politically, still less an interchange between states.

Another source of the tendency to regard international trade as a trade between states is the difference of *currencies*. The states are now the only or the chief producers of currency : and currency is generally on a different basis in every state, except where a monetary union exists.[2] All trade values are calculated in the terms of currency, and part of international trade is dependent on the exchange of one currency for another. Thus once again the state appears to be an economic unit. And yet most of international trade is not dependent upon currency

[1] *cf.* A. Marshall, " Industry and Trade," 1919, Ch. II. It is there pointed out that the only statistics of trade are as between states, but localities might equally well be regarded as economic units. The point here, however, is that there are *non-local* units in international trade ; although, of course, local units cannot be neglected.

[2] e.g. The Latin Monetary Union, the Scandinavian Monetary Union.

at all, but on *credit* and money of account which is absolutely international: therefore in this matter also international trade is seen to be rather an interchange between non-political economic groups than between peoples or states.

The figures for "foreign" trade, however, indicate how far the life of any people is bound up with international economic life. A comparison of several countries for the years 1901 and 1912 will show the interdependence of nations and the increase in that interdependence. The figures given are in English currency to the nearest £1,000.[1]

TABLE II

VALUES OF FOREIGN TRADE

	1901.		1912.	
	Net Imports.	Exports.	Net Imports.	Exports.
United Kingdom[2]	454,148	280,022	632,903	487,223
Belgium	(1906) 138,161	(1906) 111,754	198,320	158,059
France	174,768	160,516	329,232	268,504
Germany	266,500	217,900	525,700	440,400
Italy	68,240	54,978	148,077	95,877
Japan[3]	(1907) 50,477	(1907) 44,142	63,189	53,796
Netherlands	170,590	144,474	301,090	259,426
Spain	36,028	29,421	41,955	41,261
Switzerland	42,000	33,463	79,164	54,305
United States	(1903) 213,691	(1903) 290,048	344,430	452,150

As was indicated above, it is an accident of *political* development that the available statistics relate to trade crossing administrative frontiers; but statistics could be obtained of all the products, for example, of coal-mining and engineering in the whole world, balanced against all

[1] The figures are from Cd. 7527. The two earlier columns are for 1901 except where otherwise stated. Further details in regard to the figures are to be found in the sources quoted.

[2] Net imports are calculated by abstracting re-exports from total imports.

[3] Figures for General Trade.

INTERNATIONAL TRADE

the services of shipping which uses coal and engines. The selection of states, therefore, as economic units is supported seemingly by statistics; and yet nothing more is shown by them than that in certain states industries are more advanced than similar industries in other countries. The political problem results that the interests or persons in those advanced industries have peculiar relations to those to whom they export their goods. The exporters tend to "stand for" the state in its external relations: and they come into conflict with those in their own state who do not export but wish to expand the "home" market. Thus foreign policy often seems to be a mere adjustment of the claims of opposing groups of citizens.

The situation is more complicated by the introduction of obviously "international" services such as shipping and foreign investment. Thus in 1913, the United Kingdom imports were valued at £768,734,739 and the exports valued at £634,820,326 exclusive of bullion.[1] The result shows that in 1913 the United Kingdom imported goods worth about £124,000,000 *more* than the value of exports. But this only indicates another peculiarity of the United Kingdom: for in the same year there was the following additional income accruing:—[2]

Interest on Foreign Investments	£200,000,000
Freights, Services of Ships, etc.	£130,000,000
Insurance, Banking, Commissions, etc.	£ 30,000,000
	£360,000,000

Therefore it was possible not only to pay for the extra value of imports, but there was a balance of £236,000,000 to be spent or saved in the United Kingdom. But this introduces a new element into foreign policy, for it is obviously desirable for a government to promote international services which are also a source of financial gain to its own citizens.

From these and similar figures it may be seen (1) that certain nations have more international interests than others, irrespective of area and population. For example, the Netherlands is more "international" in this sense than France. It may also be argued (2) that there is a universal increase of interdependence, amounting in many cases to double the amount in ten years. Further (3) by showing the balance against any nation (imports *minus* exports)

[1] Cd. 7585. Trade for 1913.
[2] Monthly report of Barclay's Bank, October, 1919.

and by referring also to the adjustment of that balance through shipping services, interest on loans, etc., it may be proved that some nations have considerably more interest in international services than others. All such conclusions, however, must be recognised to be very inexact statements, for they and the figures to which they refer do not take account of many imponderable interests or complicated relationships. For example, Switzerland has no coal and hardly any raw materials and yet " its economic life is largely dependent upon foreign trade." [1] It has therefore extensive international interests.

The mere *amount* of " foreign " trade does not show clearly enough the character of the problem in international politics: it is necessary also to have some idea of the *character* of the goods imported and exported. Even apart from the dangers of war and blockade which may cut off a people from its food supplies, all commercial treaties and even the characteristics of diplomacy vary in accordance with the sort of goods which a people is supposed to need to import from abroad.

The kind of interdependence can be shown partly by analysing the figures for imports and exports so as to indicate which countries supply raw material or food and which supply manufactured products.

TABLE III
KINDS OF COMMODITIES IN FOREIGN TRADE
Values in £1,000 : for the year 1912.

	Foodstuffs, etc.		Raw Materials.		Manufactures.	
	Imports	Exports	Imports	Exports	Imports	Exports
U. Kingdom	265,494	32,686	208,381	59,417	156,278	385,028
Belgium ..	48,510	20,111	105,613	76,931	32,306	59,022
France ..	72,136	33,992	192,528	77,796	64,568	156,716
Germany..	157,400	39,200	289,200	116,600	79,100	284,600
Italy[2] ..	31,319	28,959	82,405	37,160	34,353	29,758
Japan[2] ..	7,359	5,616	43,095	31,395	12,370	15,898
Netherl'nds	90,635	89,949	133,042	96,844	63,152	12,772
Spain ..	6,792	17,290	20,102	13,510	15,062	10,461
Switzerl'nd	25,148	7,924	27,896	5,972	26,120	40,409
U. States[2]	88,845	87,237	117,026	223,158	75,004	140,056

[1] Report of Export Commission, p. 140.
[2] For Italy, Japan and U.S.A., raw materials are added to goods, like silk-yarn, semi-manufactured. It is difficult, especially in regard to semi-manufactured articles, to compare the figures of the several countries, e.g. chemical products may be raw material or manufactures, so may silk yarns, etc. From Cd. 7527.

From these and similar figures it may be shown that the great importers of foodstuffs before the war were the United Kingdom, Germany and the Netherlands, that the great exporters of manufactured articles were the United Kingdom, Germany and France, and that the United States stood out as a source of raw materials. It is remarkable also that the Netherlands stood so high as a source of foodstuffs, their exports being greater in value than those exported from the United States.

Policy is sometimes based upon the conception that a state should be independent of the need of foodstuffs and materials useful in war. Thus von Bülow described before the war how he tried to increase German agriculture :[1] and it seems to be accepted in England that the danger of future wars is one valid reason for artificial and uneconomic support for "key" industries.[2] Thus, optical glass is needed in war : and it might not be possible without government aid to secure that all necessary optical glass is produced within the frontiers of Great Britain. Obviously if war is likely or possible, policy must take account of it : and here the irreconcilable opposites of foreign policy are to be seen. The preparation for war by economic isolation tends to produce war by increasing the number of the interests favoured by war. The state is, therefore, at one and the same time promoting friendly trade in some commodities while it promotes war in regard to others : and this is one of the reasons why the policy of the most peace-loving Foreign Minister cannot at present be altogether favourable to peace. The only possible solution of the problem would be to make war so unlikely as to make the risk of its occurring negligible. Then foreign policy might promote the increase of international trade.

In international politics one broad distinction lies between industrialised countries and countries which are agricultural or which supply raw material. All states having colonial dependencies or possessions unite under the same government both the industrial and the raw material countries ; and an effort is sometimes made thus to secure a closed circle under the one government, supply

---

[1] "Imperial Germany," English edition, p. 209. Tariff Laws 1902. The same conception is accepted as obvious by the Agricultural Policy Committee.

[2] Report of Committee on Commercial Policy (Balfour of Burleigh), Cd. 9035 (1918).

and manufacture being in the hands of men of the same "nationality" or bearing the same allegiance. Thus the proposals of the Dominions Royal Commission seem to imply that within the British Empire the industries of the United Kingdom should be able to find all their raw material. The Commission say that in regard to articles produced outside the Empire "Government action is needed in order to promote economic independence."[1] Carried to a further point, the same policy would suggest that the markets for industrial products should also not be outside the Empire and this would secure economic "self-sufficiency." The policy is not obviously absurd when in a large empire the sources of raw material can be controlled by the will of the industrialised section of the state; for example, in spite of local advice and the views of local traders, an export tax was placed on palm-kernels from the British colonies on the West Coast of Africa, by the order of the home Government.[2] The attempt thus to create in British colonies a preserve of palm-kernels for the use of the manufacturers in the United Kingdom was followed by the prohibition of exports to foreign countries from certain French colonies, and since at present there are many of these restrictions in the case of some nations there is always ground for reciprocal segregation of resources by other nations.

The same policy of promoting the economic self-sufficiency of the political unit is adopted even by small states. It is known as "economic nationalism"; and the aim seems to be to make each small state as far as possible independent of the industries of other states. The main argument is the danger of war, since modern war is industrial and a good supply of armaments is more necessary than a healthy peasantry. The Balkan States, for example, depended upon foreign imports for the supply of their instruments of slaughter in 1912 and 1913. Not only preparation for war, however, lies at the back of economic nationalism: for there is a false social standard at work on the minds of men. It is imagined that civilisation and the status of a people is promoted by the advance to industrialism: and the industrial proletariat of large cities is regarded as more "civilised" than the peasantry of an agricultural country. The result is that peoples support governments in their attempt to build up local industries.

[1] Cd. 8462, Sect. 352. [2] *cf.* Hansard, H. of L., Dec. 17, 1919.

Apart altogether from the risk of war, government must take account of the dependence on foreign sources of food and material. No people should depend entirely on only one source for what it needs; and therefore the distribution of the dependence of one nation among a number of other nations is generally regarded as desirable. Thus if most of the wheat required in the United Kingdom came from the United States, the position would be less secure than if wheat came to the United Kingdom also from India, Egypt and the Ukraine. The supply is less likely to be seriously disturbed by any changes in one of many sources: but if all the supply comes from one source, a sudden drought or sudden industrial or political changes might cause distress in the importing country. Thus the need for many sources of supply is not based upon the danger of war, although this danger is another reason for avoiding dependence on one source. The increase in the number of sources for commodities is a normal economic phenomenon, without governmental causes. Thus cotton is now grown in U.S.A., India, Egypt and the West Indies, coffee in Brazil and Java; and therefore it is unlikely that the supply of the world will at any time be entirely interrupted. Agreed policy between governments might support and develop this tendency, for the good of all peoples.

Continuing to suppose that peoples form separate economic units, the methods should be noted by which the governments affect the economic situation, by prohibitions, tariffs, draw-backs, etc. In some cases the government desires revenue; in others it aims at national self-sufficiency, especially in view of war; in others some obscure economic belief is prevalent, as that competition between the home producer and the foreigner may be equalised by a tariff; in others it is believed that the state ought to promote trade, while " trade " is assumed to mean the business of those nationals who have political power.

Two large volumes published by the British Board of Trade indicate the activities of government for the obstruction of trade:[1] these show the tariffs in British Dominions and dependencies and in foreign countries. A knowledge of the amount payable in various countries for importing articles is essential to traders, and in some cases the amounts are so large that import from particular countries is impossible. Thus political problems arise: for there is

[1] Cd. 8094 (1915) Colonial.   Cd. 7180 (1913) Foreign.

pressure on governments from traders for (1) special agreements or treaties to overcome obstacles to trade, and for (2) reciprocal measures against foreign traders. Almost all states now obstruct trade more or less ; and so do the governments of most parts of the British Empire. It is evidently thought to be worth while : but the fact is more important than the reasons given for it. Some activities of government, then, may be taken as examples of the problems which result from tariffs. In France the State attempts to promote trade mainly by tariff manipulation. Existing duties protect agriculture, spinning and weaving, sugar and metals. In 1912 bounties for agriculture amounted to over two million francs and bounties for silk spinners to about two and a half million. Special free entry is given to articles to be worked up for export : for example, unbleached silk is brought in to be exported when dyed ; wheat is brought in to be exported as manufactured foodstuffs. A law of 1898 makes it necessary for every department to have at least one chamber of commerce, and every effort is made to maintain intimate relations between administration and commerce.

In the United States the new Tariff Law of 1913[1] reduced the existing tariffs and greatly simplified the regulations. Many articles were put on the free list, and thus trade was made easier but is still greatly obstructed. A special Tariff Commission studies the whole problem. It is to be noted, however, that *changes* in tariffs are almost as bad for trade as the tariffs themselves. Thus the power under the Canadian Anti-Trust Act to vary the tariffs in accordance with an estimate of comparative costs of production has introduced new uncertainties. In the United States one school of thought stands for the principle that tariffs ought to equalise competitive costs as between nations. This is a new problem : but it may be solved by the denial of the economic unity of separate peoples, and the consideration of industries as units. In Japan, the Government is very closely allied to trading interests.[2] The introduction of new industries such as spinning, ship building, cement, glass, etc., was contrived by the setting up of Government factories which were afterwards sold to private owners.

[1] Cd. 7128 gives this law.
[2] McGovern, "Modern Japan," 1920. It appears that not only trade but all the activities of human life are governmentalised in Japan.

A higher Council of agriculture, commerce and industry, including business men, is supported financially by the Government, and the Government sends out many special trade investigators to foreign countries.

Other instances show government action definitely in view of the dangers of war. In the United Kingdom, for example, the Admiralty in about 1905 refused to allow contractors to buy Belleville boiler tubes for British warships abroad : but only three small British firms then made them. The ships then being built were delayed but the tubes were eventually supplied in Great Britain. The chief firm supplying, however, was a German firm which set up works in Great Britain and which continued to be under German control, earning money to be spent in Germany, until during the war a British company was formed to take over the works.

The two policies of Free Trade and Protection have played a great part in the action of British Governments ; and there is some tendency in other countries to change the prevailing systems of tariff restriction in the direction of free trade. It is sometimes said that Free Trade is advantageous to Great Britain not because of any inherent good in such a principle but only because of the more advanced industrial position of the country : but in any case the international trade of the present is much more affected by the tariffs and prohibitions of Governments than by the Free Trade theory.

The instances given above suffice to show how many problems arise out of the economic status and the economic and political beliefs of the peoples of the world. In normal times a certain amount of free production and international distribution of goods does take place, but the policies of governments form a part of the organisation of world trade, and most of those policies are obstructive. " In a régime of free trade and free economic intercourse it would be of little consequence that iron lay on one side of a political frontier and labour, coal and blast-furnaces on the other. But as it is, men have devised ways to impoverish themselves and one another, and prefer collective animosities to individual happiness."[1] Such a statement indicates how political aims obstruct the enjoyment of economic wealth ; but there are results even in the political sphere which are important for international politics.

[1] Keynes, " Economic Consequences," p. 91.

The segregation of nations is an opportunity for reaction and the secret power of small groups of "interested" persons in each nation. The more difficult it is to use the produce of foreign countries, the lower the level of amenities and necessaries available for the mass of the population.[1] The supply of goods is restricted in the whole world and in each nation the prices rise. Even if the wages of favoured groups of workers also rise, the extremes of wealth and poverty are made greater by the obstacles to free interchange of goods: and the authoritarian principle, the government of the majority by a few others, is established through the control of wealth by the few. That is reaction. Again, the more restrictions there are, the more subtlety and cunning are required to avoid restrictions or to use them for private ends: hence the segregation of nations gives a new opportunity for commission agents, investment brokers, middlemen and shipping companies to coin private wealth out of their special knowledge.

The mere absence of all governmental action in regard to trade would not, however, solve all the problems. Obstacles to trade and intercourse may be made by traders themselves. Combines and agreements may restrict supplies; resources may be kept undeveloped or supplies cornered. It follows that some kind of inter-state agreement may have to be developed for the sake of controlling purely private economic interests, while separate action even for good purposes may be dangerous.

Outside the régime of tariffs and prohibitions the activity of governments is sometimes to be found in the purely financial sphere. The exchange rates may be such that prices of foreign goods are prohibitive and governments may attempt to control the exchange in favour of their own nationals. This may have unexpected consequences. Again, the manipulation of governmental loans may affect the exchanges: for example, a British Government loan was announced in New York on October 22nd, 1919, the money from which was to be used for certain liabilities. The result of the loan, it was hoped, would be to make the sovereign rise in value; but as a matter of fact the sovereign fell from $4.18½ to $4.17¼ on October 22nd. Why? Apparently, among other causes, because a third party—Scandinavian traders—sold out sterling in London in order

[1] Tariff wars occurred in 1888–1898 (France and Italy), 1890–93 (France and Switzerland), 1893–4 (Russia and Germany).

to go into dollars in New York. That is to say, that Scandinavia lent England money in New York. The financial system is sensitive internationally. The effect of the action of one government, acting separately in the world market of finance, may be such as to be detrimental to that government itself and must inevitably affect the exchange in relation to other countries. The evidence would seem to indicate that any manipulation of exchanges by governments should be under international agreement. It has been suggested that there might be an International Commission through which all governments might be informed of what is being done by any government in regard to foreign exchanges : and that no action in regard to the exchanges should be taken by any government without the cognizance of this International Commission. That would be a first step. The Commission might also organise the unofficial manipulation of the exchanges, since the development of the economic organisation of the world is not necessarily a task for governments.

Even in the case of normal trade and apart from the operations of governments in tariffs, the governments indirectly affect independent international finance because they are the sources of currency. If the currency of any nation is depreciated as compared to that of another, trade becomes difficult ; and the difficulty is greater perhaps when the values of the currencies are fluctuating, although this may be to the advantage of the speculator. Again, the reckless raising of foreign loans by unstable governments obstructs trade, and inflation of the currency either for raising loans or for paying interest on them also obstructs. It would seem, therefore, a useful part of international administration to have some international authority which could control the issue of currency and the raising of loans by sovereign states. Depreciation and inflation in one country affect the trade of the whole world ; but we are not yet sufficiently civilised to abolish in this matter the absurd independence of incompetent governments, and the governments of the chief states in dealing with their own finance have hardly proved themselves capable of improving the financial situation of other states or of the world at large.

The well-known international phenomenon of the fluctuation of prices has been the occasion of governmental action, as for example in the case of Brazilian coffee. The increase in the amount of coffee put on the market brought prices down, and the Brazilian Government therefore supports financially a Commission for buying coffee from the planters to keep it until the world price is suitable, when it is put in adjusted quantities on sale. The Government has also restricted the production of coffee: and although the action taken was clearly intended for the interest of Brazil only, it has had an international effect in restricting speculation on coffee shipments.

So many indications point to the gain of all peoples from the gradual development of international trade that it may appear natural to expect governments to act either jointly or alone for its promotion : but no government and perhaps no people can yet think of international trade except in terms of rivalry between their own foreign trade and that of another people. The Boards of Trade and Ministries of Commerce are normally thought to represent interests as opposed as those of War Ministries : and yet practice has advanced upon theory. Governments have entered into agreements for the removal of obstacles to trade.

The chief method hitherto adopted by governments for promoting foreign trade has been the commercial treaty. Such a treaty is an agreement to act in a specified way in regard to the economic relations (financial or commercial) of the nationals of the states signatory to the treaty. The most common plan involves the " most-favoured nation " clause in a treaty remitting part of the tariff in favour of this or that nation. But there are many other subjects on which governments find it necessary to agree. The validity of contracts is such a subject : and many difficulties still remain to be overcome which arise out of differences of practice in different states. Patent laws are another source of difficulty. In France, for example, an article has to be manufactured in the country before it can be patented, and therefore the foreign manufacturer to protect himself has to put up works in France. Trade marks are the subject of an international agreement ; and there is a convention in regard to copyright for literary and artistic property.

These are indications of international organisation in regard to economic supply and demand. As compared with the diplomatic connections of finance and government, the elaborate tariff restrictions and the jealousies of trading groups in the several states, international organisation by

INTERNATIONAL TRADE

governments is new and very limited in effectiveness. There is indeed hardly any conception of an *international* policy to be pursued by any government in regard to the " foreign " trade of its citizens or subjects : for even the arguments for Free Trade appeal rather to the gain to be derived from the system for the particular people who practise it. Nevertheless, the traditional philosophy of Free Trade has been connected with ideas of world peace and the amity of peoples. It has been said that the followers of Cobden expected the angel of peace to descend, clothed in untaxed calico : and although the trade now free has not brought peace, undoubtedly the conception of trade as an advantage to all parties concerned forms the only possible basis for the development of this section of international life.

(c) *Non-governmental activities*

Attention may now be directed to the operation of certain non-governmental trading interests or activities which affect international politics. These include the banking and exchange system, " foreign " investment and the formation of international combines or agreements. In normal times the production and distribution of goods is dependent upon a completely international organisation which operates in the main independently of governments.

Normal trade is facilitated by the system of bills of exchange. A bill of exchange, as everyone knows, is simply an account of money owed which is drawn out by the seller of goods, and which when signed or " accepted " by the buyer of the goods becomes a sort of international currency. The bills drawn, for example, in America for England are balanced by bills drawn in England for America : but even here the transactions are only in a superficial sense national; for the real exchange of goods and services lies between all the members of one industry (in every nation) and all the members of another. That, however, does not concern the present argument. It is sufficient if it be noted that the machinery of trade and the credit upon which that machinery rests are more truly international than is the state-system or politics. The traders of different lands really work upon the hypothesis that both parties to a transaction should gain by it : but that is not the normal practice of foreign politics; and again, the chief firms of the world are well known to one another and have a mutual credit which is not common as between governments. Thus the machinery of trade is an international fact of the first importance.

This system is worked largely through the banks; and as will be seen, the banks are so placed as to indicate, in the " undeveloped " countries at least, the character of the financial or industrial control in those countries. But when we turn to foreign investment the situation is more difficult, for politics enters in. The raising of foreign loans and the placing of investments abroad is in the hands of comparatively few financiers in every industrialised country. For example, the savings of French small farmers are drawn up to Paris; and in the banks there accumulated into large sums, which have in the past been placed in loans to Russian and Rumanian public authorities. The operations of the financial group in Paris are carried on chiefly through the Crédit Lyonnais, the Banque de Paris et des Pays Bas, the Union Parisienne and the Banque française pour le Commerce et l'Industrie; and these institutions are in close connection with diplomatic circles, aiming perhaps not at wealth but at prestige or military predominance or the maintenance of a particular kind of government. Thus, very often, the financier is simply a tool in the hands of the politician.

In the same way in London or New York small groups of financiers organise the placing of capital in other countries. All large enterprises rely on these groups for raising the requisite capital: and in some cases foreign governments approach the financiers. The governments of the lending peoples cannot afford to neglect this movement of capital; and in some cases, as in that of the Chinese Government Loan, the governments adopt a definite policy. The existence of a loan or of investment abroad creates a peculiar relation between the governments of the two countries concerned: for there are creditor and debtor nations and the government of the creditor nation has sometimes to assist in collecting debts owing not to itself, but to its citizens.[1]

The non-governmental organisation of trade, however, develops almost in independence of government action. The situation is at present to be understood, first, from a review of certain examples of the distribution of banks.

[1] *cf.* Brailsford, "War of Steel and Gold," p. 63 *seq.*, on debtor nations.

INTERNATIONAL TRADE

London has been hitherto the financial centre of world trade, and almost every bank in the world has a London bank as its agency or has itself a branch in London. London banks make a practice of developing as agents for foreign trade, a great London bank being in some cases the agent for about a hundred foreign banks in all parts of the world. There are British banks outside the British dominions, in the Levant,[1] in China, Japan and the Dutch East Indies, and all over South America.[2] The great German banks before the war, the Disconto-Gesellschaft, the Deutsche and the Dresdner Banks, operated abroad largely through subsidiary banks and by part-control of foreign banks; for example, the Disconto-Gesellschaft had stock in the Compagnie Commerciale Belge of Antwerp; the National bank für Deutschland in 1895 took shares in the Credito Italiano and supplied capital in 1909 for the Crédit Mobilier Française of Paris. In 1894 the Banca Commerciale Italiana was founded by the joint action of the Deutsche, Dresdner, Darmstadter Banks and the Disconto-Gesellschaft as well as others. In a similar manner certain great French banks control some foreign banks, and this has been the policy of the Banque de Paris et des Pays-Bas. The other two great French banks are the Crédit Lyonnais and the Société Générale; but the French banks appear as a rule to exist for the sake of investment rather than of trade in foreign countries.[3]

The banks of the United States in the past have been disconnected local units and the avoidance of the system of " branches " has limited the possibilities of American banking abroad. The situation, however, has been transformed by the Federal Reserve Act, establishing twelve reserve banks and a Federal Reserve Board to co-ordinate the banks hitherto separate. This naturally strengthens American banking for operations abroad and the Act also grants power to the banks to accept drafts

[1] Anglo-Levantine, British Oriental, Anglo-Palestine Co. For the whole of this subject, *see* Report on Co-operation in Export Trade, Federal Trade Commission, U.S.A., 1916.

[2] London and River Plate (founded 1862), 30 branches in South America; Anglo-South American, 20 branches; London and Brazilian, 18 branches; British Bank of South America, 13 branches; Commercial Bank of Spanish America, 6 branches, etc., etc. Further details in the banking number of the *Economist* (October, 1919), and the *Statist*.

[3] *cf.* Lysis, " L'oligarchie, financière," and F. Delaisi, " La Démocratie et les Financiers," 1911.

and bills of exchange. International co-operation also has begun as, for example, in the French-American Banking Corporation, including the Comptoir National d'Escompte, the National Bank of Commerce of New York and the First National Bank of Boston; and it may be that large banking combines may be formed on an international scale.[1]

The New York banks show another kind of internationalism, based upon unformulated agreements of different national institutions. Thus there is J. P. Morgan & Co., with Morgan, Grenfell & Co. of London and Morgan, Harjes & Co. of Paris; there is Lazard Frères of New York and Lazard Frères et Cie of Paris as well as Lazard Bros. of London; J. and W. Seligman & Co. of New York, with Seligman Bros. of London and Seligman Frères et Cie of Paris.

Enough has now been said to indicate the nature of the network of banking institutions; but their connection with political movements should be observed. The extent of American banking enterprise in Cuba, for example, increased greatly after the Spanish-American War. The British in Persia and Mesopotamia have a definite policy and it is therefore interesting to note that the Imperial Bank of Persia, controlled by British capital, has its head office in Teheran and eighteen branches in Persia and Mesopotamia.[2] Its chairman is Sir H. Barnes, a director of the Anglo-Persian Oil Co., and one of its directors is chairman of that company. It holds an " exclusive concession " from the Shah and has the exclusive right to issue notes. The Eastern Bank followed the success of arms, and in October, 1919, had already established branches in Amara, Bagdad, Basra City, Basra, Hillah and Mosul. The Chairman of the Anglo-Egyptian Bank said, at a General Meeting,[3] that he " remained in Cairo

[1] In connection with the operations of trading companies it is interesting to note that an agreement has been entered into by the London County and Westminster and Parr's Bank with the Portuguese Banco Nacional Ultramarino, with 26 offices in Portugal and 23 in Portuguese East and West Africa, 4 in the East, 3 in Azores and Madeira, and 9 in Brazil. The trade of Portuguese Africa before the war was in German hands. *Times*, " City Notes," February 17, 1920.

[2] Receipts for the loan of May, 1911, of the British to the Persian Government are to be paid into the Imperial Bank, which is to be the agent of the Persian Government. *cf*. No. 3, in Cmd. 300 (1919) and p. 79 above.

[3] November 25, 1919, Report in *Times*, November 26.

INTERNATIONAL TRADE

a month, and had much to do there. Lord Allenby was most kind, and although civilian travelling in Syria and Palestine was much discountenanced, gave him every facility for visiting those countries: in Palestine they were bankers to the Army of Occupation, as they were in Egypt. Before going to Palestine he had been asked by many people, clients of theirs and others, to establish branches of the bank in Syria, and he placed the matter before Lord Allenby, who entirely out of consideration for the susceptibilities of our French allies and absolutely in contradiction to the allegations made in some newspapers, did not wish them to extend their sphere of interest into Syria, while it would be said that their expansion was taking place because the country was under temporary British military control." These are indications of the connection between policy and national banks in foreign countries: but of course this is only one element in the general and obvious relationship between governmental aims and foreign trade.

The reasons for setting up branches of national banks in foreign countries are as follows: (1) *Information.*—The credit and general status of customers in a foreign country can be discovered by a local bank and information can be supplied to the exporter who may be a customer of the home branches or head office of the bank. Especially in countries with unstable conditions this may be useful. A foreign bank might give the information but would have no special interest in giving it to one trader rather than another. (2) *Extending credits.*—The bank of the exporter's national group will discount the bills of exchange issued by the customer abroad. A great part of the success of German trade before the war in the East and in South America was due to the longer credit which German traders could give with the assistance of their banks. (3) *Exchanges.*—The currencies of different countries vary: the proportion of value between the currencies is always changing. The banks, however, will make things easier by dealing with the change from currency to currency and the trader exporting likes to reduce all his assets to his own currency. Where the representatives of banks are actually on the boards of exporting companies the whole system is much more effective and this was developed very much in Germany where, for example, the directors of the Dresdner Bank were on the boards of about 200 industrial companies. A bank of the trader's own nation may also be useful in a foreign country for securing deposits paid by foreigners for goods imported from the nation to which the bank belongs.[1]

Capital abroad.—Investments in foreign countries began on a large scale in about 1850 with the growth of railways, tramways, mining and machinery. Sometimes the states borrowed, sometimes private companies; and the goods were generally bought in the states which lent the money. Agricultural countries thus became dependent upon industrial countries; and industrial countries looked for new markets in undeveloped countries to which they exported their capital. Before the war the three chief countries having capital abroad were Great Britain, France and Germany.

The money invested abroad by inhabitants of the United Kingdom amounted in the middle of 1914 to about £3,500,000,000 or more.[2] In January 1911 it was calculated that of the total of about £3,192,000,000 invested abroad 53 % was in North and South America, 16 % in Asia, 14 % in Africa, 12 % in Australasia and 5 % in Europe. Over 60 % has gone to the making of railways.[3] During the year 1919 new capital issues amounted to £237,688,780, and of this 29 millions went to British colonies, 19½ millions to foreign countries, and 1½ millions to India and Ceylon.

Besides wholly British companies, capital from the United Kingdom often controls composite companies in which some local or other foreign capital has a share. The influence of this control is, of course, directed to promote British management of the concerns established, orders for British goods and development for British banks. During the war the United Kingdom sold about one thousand million pounds' worth of foreign securities;[4] and a certain amount of British capital in foreign companies was bought out by the nationals of the countries in which

---

[1] This is the argument of the Italian paper, *Il Sole*, of October 19, 1919, in favour of setting up Italian banks in the Balkans.

[2] "Report on Export Trade," p. 71. *cf.* for the whole subject, C. K. Hobson, "Export of Capital."

[3] Sir George Paish, *Journal of R. Statistical Soc.*, January, 1911. Full details as to the number of companies abroad dominated by British capital will be found in Vol. II of the Report of the Federal Trade Commission on Co-operation in Export Trade.

[4] Keynes, p. 258.

the companies operated. French capital outside France amounted to about £1,600,000 in 1910. It is largely placed in Government loans. The large proportion placed in Russia is notorious, and its effects on French governmental policy are well known.[1]

German capital outside Germany amounted to over £1,250,000,000 in 1914, chiefly invested in Russia, Austria-Hungary, Turkey, Rumania and Bulgaria. Austro-Hungarian securities held by Germans amounted in 1912 to £197,300,000 : in Russia she had £95,000,000 in private enterprise, and in 1906 in Russian Government securities £150,000,000.[2] Belgian capital abroad in 1911 was about £108,000,000, of which in 1899 £19,000,000 was in commercial undertakings in Russia, although some of the shares may have been owned in France.[3] Switzerland has about £104,000,000 abroad, and this may be connected with the large foreign trade of Switzerland. Holland has large investments in Japan, China, the East Indies and South America.

The capital from industrialised nations flows to the non-industrialised. For example, the external debts of Russia (governmental and municipal) amounted in 1917 to £946,721,000,[4] and this excludes the foreign capital in private enterprises in Russia. South America, again, is notoriously dependent upon foreign capital.

Sometimes the fact that the capital and control is in the hands of one nation is an obstacle to the exporters or managers from another. Thus traders from the United States have complained that they cannot obtain orders because in the Argentine railways are controlled by the English, and in Chile electric light works are owned by Germans. A rivalry is thus created which may complicate the policy of governments in regard to the country in which the capital of their nationals is invested or which is desired as a market for the trade of their nationals. A larger international view would solve many such difficulties but the international view is not common.

The mere amount, however, of the capital of each nation invested within the frontiers of another nation

[1] *cf.* J. Bonzon, " La débâcle des placements Russes," 1919.
[2] Estimates are collected in Keynes, p. 162. An official and compulsory census of German securities abroad was made in 1916, but the results have not been published.
[3] Hobson, *op. cit.*, p. 156.
[4] Council of Foreign Bondholders, Report, 1918, p. 282.

will not give a sufficiently vivid idea of the present situation. Examples must, therefore, be given to show (1) the operations of foreign groups and (2) the difficulty of disentangling different national "interests" in the case of great modern companies. When capital is "exported" the foreign country may become dependent on the citizens of the lending nation not only for cash and commodities but also for the intellectual and imaginative ability necessary for organisation. Thus Italy at the beginning of the recent war found herself in a difficult financial position not only because some great banks there had been formed with German capital, but also because the banking and some of the trading organisation was largely dependent upon the ability and experience of Germans resident in Italy. A company owning property and having its national management abroad may be regarded as useful for political purposes by its home government. To take a small but definite instance, the Alby United Carbide Factories, Ltd., is a British company owning property in Norway. During the war, in 1917, the company was offered a very good price for its property by a Norwegian syndicate, but on communicating their offer to the British Government the Foreign Office indicated to the company that it would be regarded as opposed to British interests if the property passed out of their hands.[1] This clearly indicates that some political gain is derived from property in foreign countries, and it is easy to see that such companies may on the one hand bind closer together the nations concerned and on the other, in case of disagreement with local authorities, they may support opposition between the nations.

The holding of concessions in countries where the government is weak or the administration undeveloped may create a peculiar political situation; and although in the majority of cases the trading enterprise works smoothly, it is well to be aware of the differences of kind when "capital abroad" is considered. The British Platinum and Gold Corporation, for example, holds concessions in Colombia. In the Choco district they control about 300 square miles of properties "which are considered to cover vast deposits containing platinum." They have now amalgamated with the Paris (Transvaal) Gold Mines

[1] Statement of Chairman at meeting of Company in London, November 11, 1919.

INTERNATIONAL TRADE

Co., which also held concessions in Colombia. The chairman of the British company said to the shareholders: "It is unfortunate for the British Empire but quite the reverse for this Corporation that the Empire contains no platiniferous areas of any importance. But for our insight the large areas of platiniferous land which this Corporation controls would be lost to British industries or would only be available for those industries at second hand." [1] The opinion is quoted simply to show what is in the minds of those who direct such enterprises; but obviously the whole world stands to gain if, by the placing of capital and the application of ability, more commodities are available.

It is often difficult to say which "nation" controls a foreign enterprise: for example, the Huileries de Congo Belge, founded in 1911, affecting large areas in the Congo basin is controlled by Lever Brothers. Again, companies change their domicile to avoid this or that taxation: for example, the Sennah Rubber Co. transferred its offices to the Continent by a vote of shareholders.[2]

Capital abroad, however, does not always go into entirely undeveloped districts; and it may sometimes affect the daily lives of highly civilised communities. For example, the Rio de Janeiro Land, Mortgage, etc., Co., bought the holdings of two Brazilian land companies in the suburbs of Rio, and the chairman announced that there was a dearth of houses in Rio and that immigration would probably begin again.[3] Here we have an instance of a foreign company on which the simplest necessities of the locality depends; and another more famous instance is that of the drainage of the city of Rosario. A British company with £800,000 capital holds a seventy years' concession to supply drainage in Rosario in the Argentine: all householders pay for the use of the drains and the profits have allowed of a four per cent. dividend and paying interest on the debentures. The drainage of Valparaiso

[1] Report of General Meeting, London, December 30, 1919.

[2] The vote was 124 against and 12 for the removal, but the 124 represented 27,638 shares and the 12 represented 101,000. Three-quarters of the capital was held in warrants to bearer and their holders were unknown. The situation is interesting from the point of view of anyone concerned with the moral responsibility of shareholders. Details are from the Yearly Meeting, November 24, 1919.

[3] General Meeting, December 29, 1919.

also is controlled by a British Company.[1] It is calculated indeed, that the British capital invested in local public utilities in South America, exclusive of telephone companies, amounted to about £124,000,000 in 1916; but the shares of some of the concerns involved now tend to be acquired by local residents and because of the British income tax the companies may become non-British. The electrical goods used in large South American towns were largely provided by German capital which secured the largest public contracts.

A specially difficult situation arises out of such operations. The property in railways, trams, telephones and electrical works is regarded as " foreign " property: the workers sometimes strike and destroy such property and they enlist in their defence the popular sentiment adverse to foreign capitalists who control the national or local necessities.[2]

In all these cases there is a special connection between this or that enterprise and this or that nation. The several Governments are, therefore, in some sense committed by the foreign investments of their nationals and as there is a rivalry of traders, the rivals may seek to make their several governments also adopt a policy of rivalry.

The cases mentioned are examples of companies more or less national rather than international, so far as the controlling power is concerned; but there are many companies in which the control is shared between men of different nations. For example, the Zambesia Mining Development Ltd. has for its chairman (1919) Sir Alfred Sharpe, K.C.M.G., C.B., sometime Consul in Central Africa and afterwards Commissioner and Commander-in-Chief in the British Central-African Protectorate, a J.P. in Lancashire.

On the board of directors is General Paiva de Audroda " a well-known figure in the Colonial history of Portuguese Colonies, director of the Companhia da Zambesia, the Angola Mining and Prospecting Co., the Angola Diamond Co. and the Angola Petroleum Co. Another director is Dr. Bathasar Cabral, vice-governor of the Banco Nacional Ultramarino. Another director, Mr. Libert Oury, is on

[1] cf. Davies, " The State in Business," and the *Stock Exchange Year Book*, 1919.

[2] cf. The Press generally in regard to Argentine Railway strikes of 1919.

INTERNATIONAL TRADE

the boards of the Mozambique Co., the Mozambique Industrial and Commercial Co., the Beira Railway Co., the British Central Africa Co., the Shire Highlands Railway, Nyasaland, the Central African Railway, the Beira-Zambesi Railway, and the Sena Sugar Factory. Another director, Mr. L. R. Lewis, is a director of Lysberg Ltd., and also agent for the Duffryn Rhondda Collieries, etc., and " the Coal Controllers' direct representative for export in the British Channel." The Zambesia Mining Development Co. have now (1919) the whole mineral rights of an area of 35,000 square miles, containing coal, gold, copper, iron and mica.[1]

The Mozambique Company, of which Sir A. Sharpe is President of the directors in London, and Mr. L. Oury is manager, "acquired a charter from the Portuguese Government granting *sovereign rights* over a territory of about 60,000 square miles in South East Africa. The company's revenue is mainly derived from customs receipts, native and other taxes, and from granting land, mining and other concessions."[2]

The Forestal Land, Timber and Railways Co. controls the production of quebrocho extract and logs in Argentine, owns five million acres of land, 200 miles of railways and some river tugs. It acquired the New York Tanning Co. in 1914, and had entered some years previously into an alliance with Renner and Co., who controlled nearly all the extract factories in Germany, Austria, Russia and France. In the Forestal Company the distribution of shares in the hands of various nationalities in 1915 was:—1,325,000 English, 866,000 German, 400,000 French, 386,000 United States, and 86,000 Dutch, besides about 36,000 shares in the hands of other nationalities.[3]

These are, of course, only slight indications of the complexity of modern investment and of the impossibility of distinguishing "national interests" by frontiers, or the names of directors, or any other simple method. Governments, therefore, which may be incited to rivalry by rival national traders may be incited to alliance by the traders of different nations who have joint interests.

There are all stages of development in these non-national companies, from a sharing of control between two or

[1] Report of General Meeting, London, November 18, 1919.
[2] *Stock Exchange Year Book*, 1919, p. 2,151.
[3] Speech of Chairman, June 8th, 1915.

three nations to a control vested in one nation while the shares are distributed among many.

The United States Steel Corporation is in the main American; but the foreign holdings show its international character. On March 31, 1914, foreign holdings were 25·3 % of the Common Stock and 8·7 % of the Preferred Stock, and it is noticeable how during the war the foreign, and especially the British, holdings decreased.[1]

	AMOUNTS IN THOUSANDS OF SHARES.				
Dec. 31st,	1914.	1915.	1916.	1917.	1918 (June 30)
Common Stock :					
United Kingdom	719	360	193	173	174
Holland	343	239	234	229	229
France	65	50	30	30	29
Canada	54	38	32	42	46
Total	1,181	687	489	474	478
All Foreign Countries	1,193	697	503	484	491 = 9·7%
Preferred Stock :					
United Kingdom	194	164	52	41	40
Holland	29	26	25	25	25
France	37	33	28	26	26
Canada	24	36	36	36	42
Total	294	259	141	128	133
All Foreign Countries	309	275	156	140	149 = 4·1%

In all these cases, then, the " interests " of the different national groups are interwoven and it is obvious that foreign policy cannot in this matter be based upon the crude hypothesis that the interests of each nation are opposed to those of others. Indeed, if governments are concerned at all with capital abroad, it is clear that they should substitute an international for a foreign policy in regard to it.

The most important fact, however, of international trade in regard to international politics is the existence of large international combines or trusts which control the whole or most of the production of a commodity in the whole world. The development of combines and trusts is one of the normal results of the modern organisation of trade and finance, and most of the combines

[1] Figures from Reports of the Corporation.

INTERNATIONAL TRADE

are still confined within national frontiers so far as their production is concerned; but even then national combines or amalgamations affect the international situation because they are much more powerful in the world market than the older, single and separate firms. Especially when a tariff wall exists an amalgamation can grow up, for foreign competition is kept out and agreement is more easily reached or financial operations more easily arranged between men of the same nation and locality. The tariff, it is said, is the mother of trusts : and when trusts or combines exist they do their best to support their mother. These, however, are largely the concerns of domestic politics. International politics is only affected in so far as international trade is obstructed and therefore international life is diminished.

The agreement, amalgamation or combination of trading interests has not been hindered by frontiers. There are increasing numbers of always more powerful international combines : and some of these already have more power than many governments. Therefore some examples may be given of the formation of these new economic units.

The international rail syndicate was formed in 1883. The members were all the seventeen or eighteen firms except one in Great Britain, all in Germany except two and Belgian firms. The markets were allotted and prices at once raised from £4 to £4 13s. per ton. The " pool " was dissolved for a time: but in about 1900 the old association was revived and in Nov. 1904 an agreement was signed between the rail makers of Great Britain, Germany, Belgium and France, each group being left in control of its own country, while the export trade was divided in proportion, the British works getting 53·5 %. In July 1905 the United States firms joined in, being probably given the American continent as market. The prices rose from £4 10s. a ton in Jan. 1905 to £5 17s. 6d. in December and to £6 12s. 6d. a ton in December 1906.[1]

A looser form of combination is to be found in the prewar metal buying combination, of which some indication is given in the appended diagram. Another example is in the oil trade. The Shell Transport and Trading Co. (1897) bought oil lands in Dutch Borneo and then entered into alliance with the Royal Dutch Petroleum Co. Other companies were absorbed, and in 1906 a holding company

[1] Macrosty, " Trust Movement," p. 63 *seq.*

THE INTERNATIONAL METAL BUYING COMBINATION (1916).
ADAPTED FROM THE REPORT ON CO-OPERATION IN AMERICAN EXPORT TRADE.

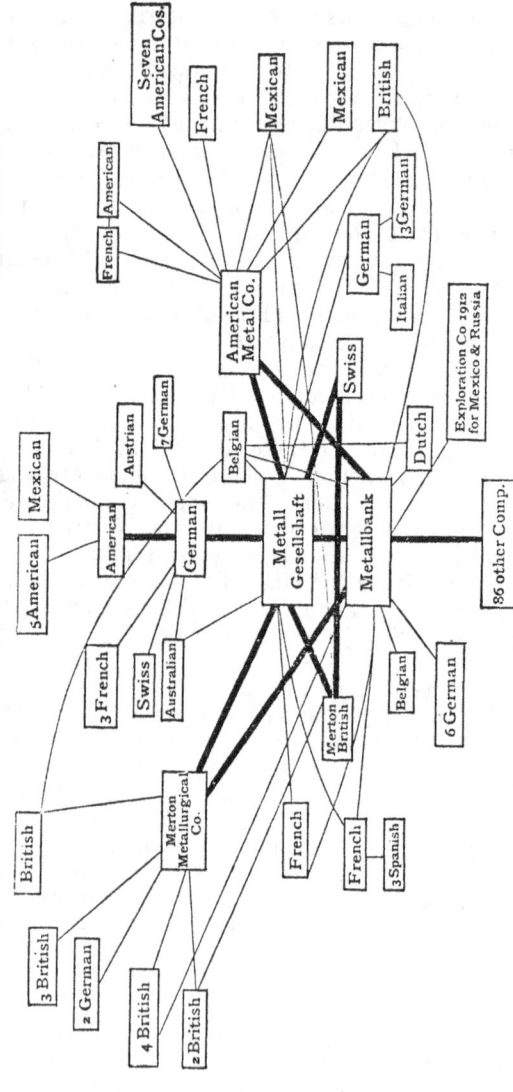

═══ = Affiliation through Stock.
──── = Ownership or interlocking directorates.

The nationality of the companies is given, and in some cases a number of separate companies are in the same enclosure.

INTERNATIONAL TRADE

was formed in which the Dutch Company took 60 % and the Shell 40 % of the shares, while the Dutch Company also took 25 % of the ordinary shares in the Shell Co.[1] Through control of the Mexican Eagle Oil Company the same group may come into important international relations with the dominant group of the United States, the Standard Oil Company. The Royal Dutch Shell group is acquiring new interests in Rumania and the Dutch Indies and has struck a new well in Tarakan near Dutch Borneo.[2]

Other examples are Borax Consolidated (Ltd.), 1899, which controls the borax production of Asia Minor and a large part of that of U.S.A., Chile and Peru : and the Chilean Iodine Company which controls most of the world's supply of iodine, and is said to restrict production in order to keep the price remunerative.

A more important instance is that of the meat supplies of most of the world which are controlled by five U.S.A. Companies, known as " the Big Five "—Swift and Co., Armour and Co., Morris and Co., Wilson and Co., and the Cudahy Packing Co. These companies are said to control jointly or separately 574 other companies, they are said to have representation on 956 other directorates and have interests in various large banks.[3] The Federal Trade Commission reported in 1918 that there was what amounted to joint action between the Big Five in purchase in U.S.A. and Argentine and in the sale of products. On the other hand, the evidence offered in behalf of Armour and Co., seems to show that the similar actions taken by the different companies is the natural result of several groups following the same trade.[4] The Board of Trade Report on Meat Supplies suggests that there is now no need for the companies to combine as a tacit agreement exists.[5] For the purpose in view here, however, it is immaterial whether there is one combine or not : for it is clear that (1) the Big Five have 86 per cent. of the live stock slaughtered in U.S.A. ; (2) in 1911 an agreement was made between the Big Five and certain British and Argentine

[1] Macrosty, p. 106.
[2] *cf.* Report of Sub-Committee on Oil Trade, Comd. 597 (1920).
[3] Report of Federal Trade Commission on the Meat-packing Industry, 1918.
[4] H.R. 13324, House of Representatives : testimony, January 21, 1919.
[5] Cmd. 456, Sect. 16.

interests in Argentina to control the meat supplies there. This "pool" disappeared in 1913, but a new agreement was made in June 1914, at meetings held in London. (3) The Allied Governments agreed to purchase meat supplies together and not in competition, and they met with what was practically only one seller. The seller was the Big Five, who could charge almost any price and could force the live-stock producers to take anything. The actual result was apparently a profit of about 100 per cent. in the year 1917. The import of meat to the United Kingdom, from Argentine has long been subject to a Trade agreement for a share of the spoils; but the share of the Big Five is increasing. In 1909 British Companies had 37 %, Argentine Companies 27·7 % and American 35·3 %. In April 1919 the output was for old British Companies 18·5 %, a new partly British Company 16·1, the only Argentine Company left 8·2 % and the American Companies 57·2 %. In 1913, the American Companies supplied half of the total import of beef to the United Kingdom. It is to be noted that not only meat but also leather, lard and innumerable by-products are controlled in the same way and that the persons in control are financial magnates and, except in the case of the banking interests,[1] these persons belong to a few United States families.

Further examples are superfluous. The tendency is to increase the number of international amalgamations and combines; but even before the war it was ascertained that—" In one way or another the world's trade in rails, tubes, nails, screws, sewing thread, bleaching-powder, borax, nitrates and tobacco is to a greater or less degree brought under international control, while at least till lately dynamite was so controlled and repeated efforts have been made similarly to syndicate the whole steel trade."[2]

Some sections of trade and finance are obviously international in their character such as telegraphy and wireless, insurance and re-insurance, but one important international service, shipping, deserves special mention.

[1] The Guaranty Trust Co. (with J. P. Morgan & Co.), the Chase National Bank, etc., entered in at the time that the British Government fear of German interests forced Sulzberger & Co. to become Wilson & Co.

[2] Macrosty, p. 342, cf. Appendix on International Combines in the Report of the Committee on Trusts, Cd. 9236 (1919), p. 40.

INTERNATIONAL TRADE

Here too, organisation has produced larger units and the great liner companies of the modern world largely control the conditions of overseas trade. The service rendered by ocean-going ships is obviously international and clearly the ship's flag does not indicate the interests in her cargoes: indeed, a great part of British shipping before the war never entered British ports but plied between the ports of other nations.

Organisation on an international scale resulted in the formation of international " conferences" or agreements as to fixed freight-rates on certain routes. The method of controlling the situation was by deferred rebates, the merchant who tried to ship by an " outside " line or ship being made to forfeit his rebates: but what is most interesting for the present purpose is that the agreement to control bound together companies of many nationalities. The main Conference in the Far East trade, for example, consisted of the P. and O. Ocean Steamship Co., Messageries Maritimes, North German Lloyd, Nippon Yusken Kaisha, Glen, Shire, Ben, Shell, Mutual and Mogul Companies;[1] agreement also bound to rules made by this Conference the lines of other nationalities including the East Asiatic Co. of Copenhagen, the East Asiatic Co. of St. Petersburg, the Hamburg-America Line, the Nederland Line, the Rotterdam Lloyd and the Compagnia Trasatlantica. Here is a complete internationalism if only for a very limited purpose.

The shipping of the world however is still regarded as essentially divided into nationalities, chiefly because of war and the danger of war; for in peace and in normal trade the shipping managers commonly regard their position as in some sense international: shipping rates cannot very well vary in accordance with nationality; and although some governments have attempted artificially, by bounties and apart from mail subsidies, to increase the shipping of their flags,[2] the open road of the ocean and the flow of international trade must prevail against any sectionalising of ocean-going shipping. Agreements have been reached internationally as to deck-loads, safety at sea, signalling, etc., and in fact every ship at sea follows an international rule.[3]

[1] Cd. 4668 (1909), Commission on Shipping Rings, p. 21.
[2] Cd. 6899 (1913), Bounties and Subsidies to Shipping in Foreign Countries.
[3] *cf.* L. S. Woolf, " International Government," p. 171.

The growth of international trade organisations, some of which are combines, trusts or shipping conferences, is obviously a matter of concern to all governments. It is a fundamental problem of international politics: for although some advantages result from the larger organisations, such power in the hands of private persons and small international groups may very well need supervision. It is sufficient here, however, to point out the need: but it may also be noted that the substitution of governmental for private trade enterprise would perhaps have undesirable consequences. Thus the chairman of the Orient Steam Navigation Co. said at a general meeting: "If international trade is to become the province of Governments and state is to trade with state, every transaction, however trivial, will contain the germ of a possible difference, the occasions of international discord will be indefinitely multiplied and in the last resort there will be no Court of Appeal except the appeal to force."[1] It is obvious that this is an argument against nationalisation which may or may not be valid according to the character of the state and the nature of international political organisation. Obviously also the argument does not hold as against a non-governmental internationalisation of shipping as a public service: but it is true that the entry of government into industry does prejudice the position of government in the pursuit of justice. The need for consideration of the problem of public service has been urged on account of the fluctuation of freight-rates for wheat affecting the business of American farmers and the food of Europe.[2] The Allied Maritime Transport Council has shown the possibility of an allocation of tonnage according to need on an international scale; and it should not be impossible in the case of this great international service of shipping to re-organise on a basis rather of public utility than private profit.

So far reference has been made chiefly to deliberate organisation of international trade and finance: but it is a fact of fundamental importance that some of the most important phenomena of international trade are not the results of design. Such for example is the case

[1] General Meeting, London, December 30, 1919.
[2] Mr. D. Lubin of the International Institute of Agriculture is the protagonist. He urges an International Commerce Commission, cf. No. 35 (1919), Institute of Agriculture.

CHART II.

CHART SHOWING THE FLUCTUATIONS IN SPECIAL IMPORTS AND SPECIAL EXPORTS DURING THE YEARS 1903-1912 IN CERTAIN COUNTRIES.

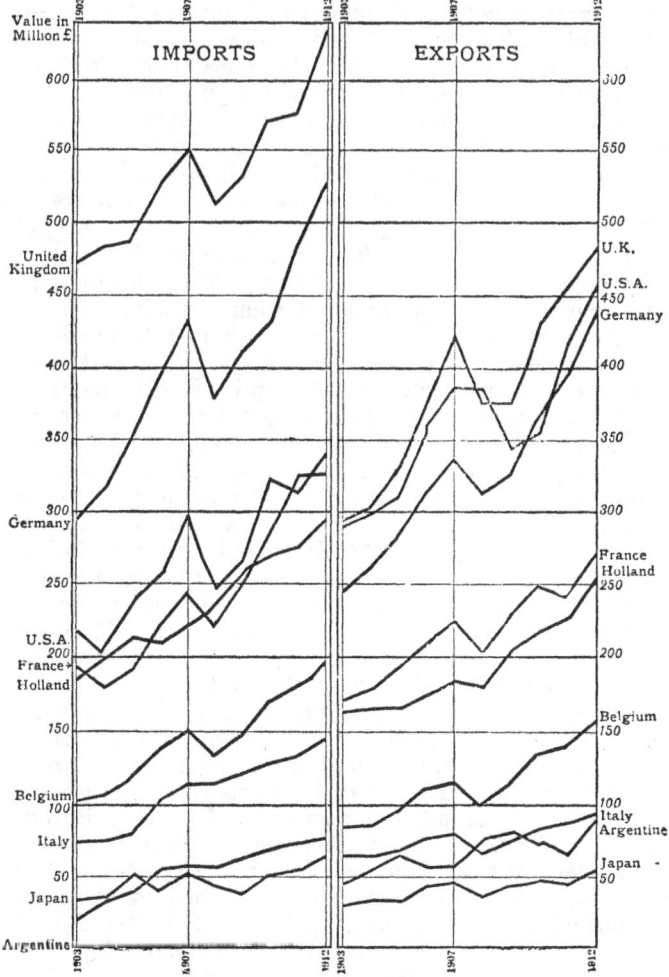

FIGURES in *Cd.* 7525.

in regard to the periodical or cyclical fluctuations of world trade. There are well-marked changes in export and import, in output of commodities, in rates of dividend, etc., which affect similarly all civilised nations. Whatever the cause of the fluctuation, it seems at present to be inevitable that fluctuations should occur, and although it may not be desirable to destroy the rhythm of trade it may very well be wise to collect and publish information on an international scale which will prevent the most dangerous forms of speculation. Governments in this matter may be the best instruments for the supply of such information; and from the accompanying chart it may be seen how useful a comparison of the fluctuations of economic life in the different countries might be.

The depression of international trade in 1908 is noticeable. In 1907 a crisis occurred in the banks of the United States and industry was at once deprived of the requisite capital. It is said that about 25 per cent. of the persons employed before the crisis were left unemployed. Hours were lessened and the government took steps to discourage immigration. The effect in England was the crisis in the cotton industry, owing to the decrease in imports of American cotton. In 1908, many industries in France, Belgium, Germany and Sweden were seriously affected, and the amount of production as well as the amount of imports and exports considerably decreased. This was an exceptional crisis; but there is a normal fluctuation in the production and trade of all countries, which seems to be due to the international character of modern finance and commerce.[1] Indeed apart from fluctuations it appears probable that the movement of prices throughout the world is similar, as may be indicated in the accompanying charts of index numbers of food-prices in Europe and elsewhere. It should be obvious then from the phenomena of trade and commerce that the international interests of any people cannot be attained by the mere conflict of contending foreign policies. The international point of view is necessary even for understanding and still more for dealing with finance and commerce.

These economic facts indicate the following problems in international policy, besides those already mentioned.

[1] Wesley Mitchell, " Business Cycles," *cf.* also the Report on " Unemployment " of the International Organising Committee, p. 12, and the chart appended.

CHART III.

INDEX NUMBERS OF FOOD PRICES.

From *Cd.* 6955 (1913).

1900 = 100 for each country. The amounts are not comparable but only the fluctuations.

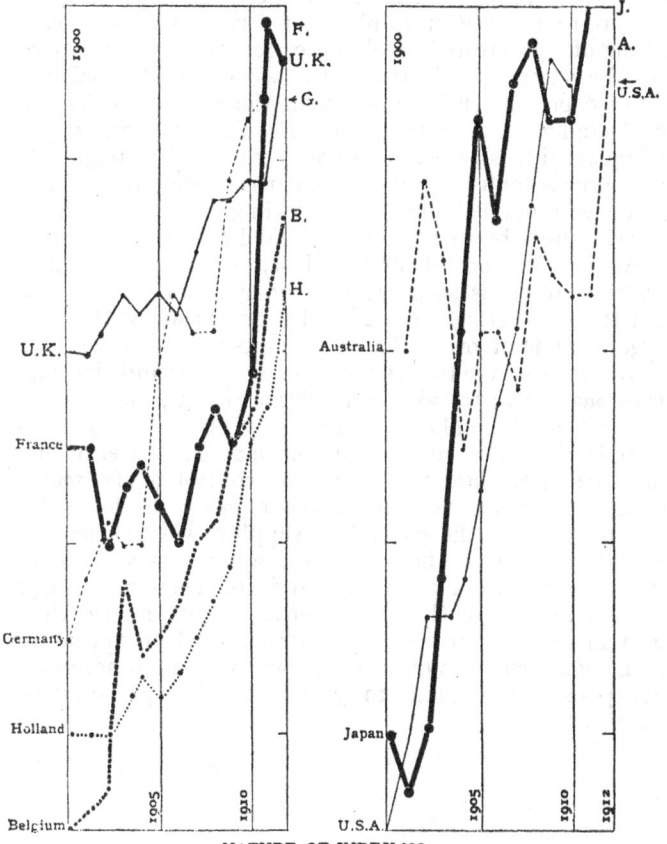

NATURE OF INDEX NO.

U.K.—Retail prices of 23 articles of food in London, weighted.

FRANCE.—Retail prices of 24 articles of food (including wine), fuel, etc., in Paris, weighted.

GERMANY.—Retail prices of 13 articles of food in Prussia, Bavaria, Baden and Wurtemberg, weighted.

HOLLAND.—Retail prices of 23 articles of food in 6 principal towns, unweighted.

BELGIUM.—Retail prices of 11 articles of food in 16 principal towns, weighted.

AUSTRALIA.—Retail prices of 41 articles of food (besides soap, starch, candles, kerosene) in 6 capital cities, weighted.

JAPAN.—Wholesale prices of 20 articles of food in 19 to 25 towns, unweighted.

U.S.A.—Retail prices of 15 articles of food in 39 principal cities, weighted.

There is a tendency for the larger industries to approach organisation on an international scale. The economic unit of the future will perhaps therefore be not local but one world-industry as contrasted with other world-industries. We need, therefore, in international politics, not a mere representation of places or states but a representation of " interests." All those, for example, who live by the shipping industry in the whole world should be able to present their views to all those who live by the coal industry. International organisation cannot be adequate if it is based only upon territorial sovereignties : and a mere conference of state or parliamentary representatives will not be suitable for dealing with the complex relationships between industry and industry.

Again, the control exercised by those who direct a world-combine is so great that no one government can master it. Perhaps it can only be mastered by the organisation of other *industrial* units ; but so long as governments have to assist in providing food and clothing, they may have to take joint action for the control of international combines. Obviously the problem is complex : for a combine of incompetent governments may be more disastrous than the control of far-seeing financiers. Some solution, however, has to be found for the problem of the control of supplies with a view to private profit : and here again the solution may be found in an organisation of finance and commerce for public service independently of the governments rather than in a mere transference to governments, which appear to be incompetent enough in their own spheres, of activities in spheres unfamiliar to popular and representative politicians.

PART II

INTERNATIONAL ORGANISATION

INTRODUCTION

IT has so far been shown that the peoples of the world enter into many different relationships, one with the other. The present complex situation is due to a gradual development, most of which was undesigned ; for although traders and travellers have brought nations into closer contact and although every man in any civilised community now depends upon foreigners for some of his food and clothing, the existing international situation is not the result of any consistent plan and is still not commonly considered or understood. Meantime the same movement goes forward : the governments are brought more and more closely into contact, the resources of the world are more widely used and by more various peoples, foreign trade increases and the scientific, artistic and religious ideas of every people are more closely interwoven with those of others.

The whole of this complexity of political, cultural and economic relations has been the result of the reaching out of the different peoples from different centres. Each group has been moved by its own needs ; and hence international politics appears in its simplest form to be a conflict of interests. The machinery for advancing those interests is, in the first place, a system of diplomatic and consular representatives of each state within the frontiers of the others. These officials are conceived to be concerned chiefly with the separate interests of their native country and at periodic conferences they seek to promote such interests in opposition to others.

A new system, however, of an international character has been developing. Men of different nations have met together not simply to gain each his own interest, but for common consultation on joint interests ; and the result has been the establishment of international organisations of various types. Here we have not merely the accidental results of a contact of separate units, but a beginning of a new social structure. Some international organisation, as for example the Universal Postal Union, is governmental and some is voluntary or unofficial; and the governmental internationalism is closely connected with the diplomatic system, while the unofficial is more various and represents a more vigorous initiative in international politics. International organisation of all kinds is the machinery by which the solution of the problems of international politics is attempted; but every civilised government has attempted separately to solve some of the problems of international politics, and therefore it cannot be truly said that these problems are to be solved only by international action. In general it may be said that diplomacy is the attempt to solve problems of frontiers, nationality, law and comparative political power. For solving economic problems there are international Socialist or Labour congresses and societies which deal with the common interests of workers in many lands: there are also international combines and trade arrangements through which trade rivalries are sometimes avoided. Again, in the cultural sphere there are innumerable international conferences and societies for religion, science and art. These all form the primitive machinery so far developed for dealing with international politics on an international scale and these, therefore, must be studied in further detail.

CHAPTER VI

DIPLOMACY

EVERY civilised state has at least one administrative office which deals with its relations to other states. The Ministers or Secretaries in control hold their powers on very different bases.[1] In autocratic states the Foreign Minister holds his position at the pleasure of the monarch, as was the case in Tsarist Russia and in Germany until November 1918. In the United States the President is more powerful than the Secretary of State even in negotiations and in France also the President seems to have very extensive powers in foreign affairs. In Great Britain the sovereign has been more active in foreign policy than in other sections of politics and this has limited the power of the Foreign Secretary.

In some cases, as in Great Britain, the office of Foreign Minister is passing through a stage intermediate between that familiar in autocracy and that usually connected with democracy. The British Foreign Secretary has to answer questions in Parliament; he is supposed to give an occasional account of action taken and presumably, if Parliament disapproved of his policy, the principle of joint Cabinet responsibility might induce a Government to dismiss him or to change his policy, unless the Government itself were compelled to resign. But apart from crises, the Foreign Secretary is, in the normal exercise of his duty, isolated and must initiate or take action often on his own responsibility; for he has not to administer laws but to negotiate. This is one instance of the larger political problem of the control of the executive.[2]

---

[1] The names, of course, vary. The British Foreign Secretary corresponds to the French Minister, the U.S.A. Secretary of State (their Foreign Office being "the State Department"), and under the old régime the German Chancellor was a Minister for foreign affairs.

[2] *cf.* Ponsonby, "Democracy and Diplomacy," esp. p. 45 *seq.*, Ed. of 1915.

Political development and political thought have hitherto been concentrated chiefly upon the problems of legislation and the representative system : and while these have been democratised, the administration of most countries is still based upon the ancient practice of autocracy in which the agent or official is the passive instrument and the people governed are supposed to leave all judgment to their rulers. In "foreign affairs," however, legislation has no importance, since laws carry only as far as frontiers ; and the representative system has little bearing on foreign policy. Executive action and the responsibility of agents are the chief problems ; and precisely these have not gone through democratisation. Therefore particularly in regard to foreign policy our systems of government are primitive.

In some nations special methods have been adopted for reforming the system. The French Chamber since 1902 has had a permanent Committee on Foreign Affairs, Protectorates and Colonies ;[1] and under the rules of procedure all proposed treaties must be referred to it. In practice the Committee is unable to control the making of agreements or to interfere in the course of negotiations ; but it is able to secure information which could not be made absolutely public ; and the Minister of Foreign Affairs may be helped by having the criticism and suggestions of the Committee if he asks for them. The position of the President of the Republic, however, still remains much more autocratic in regard to foreign policy than in any other sphere.[2]

The Constitution of the United States says that the President shall have power " with the advice and consent of the Senate " to make treaties, provided two-thirds of the Senators present concur ; and " he shall nominate and, by and with the advice of the Senate, shall appoint ambassadors, other public ministers and consuls." [3] Thus the Senate has some control over the appointment of officials ; and it has a very effective control over the making of treaties. But perhaps the most important fact, from the present point of view, is that the Senate

[1] This is one among sixteen permanent Committees of the Chamber.

[2] So, at least, a President who has performed some astonishing diplomatic feats asserts in his own book. *cf.* " How France is Governed," by R. Poincaré, Eng. trans., p. 181.

[3] Constitution of 1787, Section 2 (2).

has power to overlook and to control the Executive in its foreign policy in such a way as cannot be paralleled in any other state. The President, nevertheless, retains great power and there is no responsibility of the Executive such as in Great Britain.

The normal machinery through which the governments communicate is the Diplomatic System, which belongs by origin and by character to the late Renaissance. The Foreign Offices of the several states have different traditions: but nearly all are affected by the more primitive conceptions of state sovereignty which were in vogue in the days of Grotius. Some Foreign Offices, as for example that of Great Britain, are dominated if not entirely staffed by the minor aristocracy:[1] others, like that of France, are more closely connected with finance: others, like the State Department at Washington, are connected with law and journalism. Not unnaturally a particular class tends to be predominant in the Foreign services; for the duties of these services differ from those of other departments of government more than the work of those departments differs among themselves. The Foreign Office represents the whole state and therefore may need a particular type of training and outlook in its officials. And again, the aristocrat belongs to an international caste: and so does the financier and the journalist: for members of these castes in every nation know individual foreigners of their own caste. Further, in the duties of a Foreign service personality counts for more than in the case of other departments in which administrative routine is more prevalent: and therefore in every state the officials of the Foreign services tend to be taken from a particular class or type.

Examples of the general character of state organisation for contact with other states and peoples may be found in the British system: but it should be recognised that in choosing these examples it is not implied that the system is the best.

The British Foreign Office dates from 1782 and in 1796 it consisted, under the Secretary of State, of two under-Secretaries and twelve other officers. In 1861 it consisted of forty-four officers and in 1914 of fifty officers.[2]

[1] Commission on Civil Service, Report, Cd. 7748. About 67 per cent. of the successful candidates for attachéships came from Eton in the years from 1908 to 1913.
[2] This of course excludes second division or staff clerks."

The recruitment of the staff has been under discussion, and it is now an accepted policy that (1) the two services at home and abroad shall be more closely co-ordinated and (2) the services shall be open to men of ability of any social rank or income.[1]

A new department, the Department of Overseas Trade, was established in 1917 under the joint supervision of the Foreign Office and the Board of Trade. It has taken over the old Commercial Intelligence department of the Board of Trade and is chiefly concerned with the promotion of British trade abroad, largely by the collection and dissemination of information.[2]

The services of the state in contact with other states are further organised in the Ambassadorial system. Permanent Ambassadors or Residents were appointed by Great Britain for the first time in the middle of the seventeenth century, and were paid until about 1830 out of the personal resources of the sovereign. It was not till 1869 that Parliamentary control was secured over the Diplomatic Service by the transfer of the expenses to the ordinary Votes. There were in 1914, nine Embassies, thirteen Missions of the first class, seventeen of the second class and two Ministers Resident.[3] The staffs of the Embassies and Missions include 13 Counsellors, 12 Second and First Secretaries, 24 Third Secretaries and an indefinite number of unpaid permanent attachés. It has been the practice to transfer secretaries and attachés after a residence of two years at any Embassy or Legation in order to give them as wide an experience as possible; and this may indicate a dim understanding of the nature of international politics as contrasted with foreign politics.

[1] Cd. 7748. Recommendations of the Committee taken as basis of reform in Lord R. Cecil's speech, Hansard, H.C., 31/7/1918. *cf.* also Sir A. Steel Maitland in *Times*, May 22, 1919. Sir E. Satow fears that the old will be better (*cf.* " Diplomatic Practice," Vol. I, p. 183). The first qualifications he desires are " good temper, good health and good looks." He even seems to prefer the old rule that a candidate shall have £400 a year of his own.

[2] Cmd. 319 (1919), Report of Committee on Machinery for Trade and Commerce. Sect. 20 recommends the transfer of the Consular and Commercial Departments of the Foreign Office. Appendix B gives an account of Departments and War Departments for Foreign Trade.

[3] Cd. 7748 (1914) Report, and Cd. 7749, Evidence, Commission on Civil Service.

[4] The Ambassador at Paris gets £11,500, at Washington £10,000 a year, and others £5,000 to £8,000.

The Consular Service of Great Britain is kept distinct from the Diplomatic, although transfers are occasionally made. There are three divisions of the service, the General Consular Service, the Levant Service (for the late Ottoman Empire, Greece, Persia and Morocco) and the Far Eastern Service (for China, Japan and Siam). The office of Consul was first instituted in the fifteenth century and consuls were first required where the local government did not adequately protect life and property or where local customs were very different from the British. Consuls were for a long time local merchants engaging in trade, sometimes receiving British salaries: but the Consular Act of 1825 established the present system under which all salaried officials are forbidden to engage in trade. There are, however, still some British vice-Consuls in places where there are few British interests who are not paid and who are not of British nationality.

The practice of diplomacy has been roundly abused by many politicians and a diplomatist is commonly believed to be a professional liar.[1] Certainly the early books connected with foreign policy and diplomacy do not express any high moral code. Machiavelli has a bad name although he only analysed the frauds which many admired persons were practising. François de Callières teaches politeness to diplomatists, while indicating how to bribe spies.[2] These are indications of an evil tradition; but the excellent and progressive work done by diplomatists should not be forgotten; for indeed the moralising of the contact of nations owes more to the despised diplomats than to all the warriors whose monuments are to be seen in our cities. The normal work of an ambassador or envoy is in communications as to agreements or in the smoothing of difficulties between his own country and that in which he resides. He is the agent of a sovereign state in contact with other states: and in every great capital there is a diplomatic corps representing all the chief states of the world. The purpose of the organisation is to bring the states and through them the peoples into closer contact: and one might think that each diplomatic corps in any capital was an embryo

[1] Sir Henry Wotton's phrase is: "An ambassador is one sent to lie abroad for his country."

[2] "De la mainère de negocier avec les souverains," Paris, 1716, trans. by A. F. Whyte, under the title "The Practice of Diplomacy," 1919, see p. 26: "No expense is better designed or more necessary than that which is laid out on spies."

international administration; for it would be quite possible for all the envoys at any capital to consider jointly all issues of international importance. Unfortunately, however, the diplomatic corps is rather a fashionable society than a political unit, and the problem which seems to be regarded as of most importance in regard to the corps is the trivial question of precedence at functions.[1] At certain crises indeed envoys at a capital do act together as a body; but there is no reason why even in normal procedure some advance should not be made in internationalising the practice of the diplomatic corps in each capital. The chief obstacle is, of course, the absence of the international mind both in Foreign Ministers and in their agents abroad; for each ambassador still tends to think of the interests of his country as though they were opposed to all others. It needs, however, only one more step to make each capital a centre of practical international co-operation. It is now admitted formally that a third state can offer its "good offices" to two other governments in a dispute and "mediation" is a well-tried practice.[2] These are beginnings of real international politics.

To speak now of the envoy of each state separately, certain customs may be noted. The envoy communicates to a Foreign Minister in the country to which he is accredited either in the envoy's language or in French: and the Minister replies in his own language. The communications are either a formal "note" or a "note verbale," unsigned and in the third person, or an informal memorandum. There are elaborate rules, some international, some peculiar to this or that capital, which constitute a sort of code of good manners for envoys.[3] The envoy may be unwelcome[4] to the Government to which he is accredited and his own Government may, therefore, be induced to recall him. More important still is the legal status of an envoy. He is immune from certain legal processes in the country in which

---

[1] *cf.* Satow, "Diplomatic Practice," Vol. I, Ch. xxiii: an excellent plan is given on p. 352 of the way to arrange seats at table. The story of the quarrel of the ambassadors of Spain and France about precedence is told in Foster's "Practice of Diplomacy."

[2] *See* below, p. 146.

[3] For all details see Sir E. Satow's "Guide to Diplomatic Practice," which is chiefly concerned with good manners. It does not discuss the nature of the state in its external relations nor the development of moral action.

[4] *Persona non grata* is the phrase.

he resides, he and his official residence are exempt from taxation, and his official residence is regarded as outside the territory of the state to which he is accredited. This position is traditional and arises from the early conception of sovereignty, since the envoy in most cases represents a sovereign state. But the actual power of the envoy has been changed by modern developments.

The speed of the post and the telegraph make it possible now for the envoy continually to consult his Government: therefore he has less responsibility and also less freedom. Often the principals, the Foreign Ministers, communicate directly and not through their envoys: and while diplomacy has thus lost something of its sphere for originating or controlling policy, the result has been good in making policy more consistent in different countries and in compensating for any defects of a particular envoy. The strong man is perhaps somewhat limited but the weak man is strengthened and the whole system is made more efficient.

The staff of an embassy or mission has special functions in extension of those of their chief. Apart from direct subordinates, there are often military and naval attachés, who report to their own home departments and whose office embodies the old idea of the state as a military unit. They look out for allies and enemies, pick up information or give hints to friends. It is the simplest form of tribal contact. To them is now added in some cases a Commercial attaché, who reports upon foreign industry or commerce or markets abroad and is somehow related to a Ministry of Commerce or a Board of Trade: but he too generally looks out for special advantages for traders of his own country. This is a little more than tribal; it is Phœnician. A new stage, however, appears to have been reached in the appointment by Sweden and Finland of Social attachés, who are not to look out for advantages but to report to their Ministries of Labour any problems or solutions in the social and industrial field. Clearly here the agent of the state represents a more civilised view of the state; for it is actually to the interest of each Ministry of Labour that social and industrial conditions should be improved in every foreign country, if even for the selfish reason that it adds to the cost of production abroad! The advent therefore of Ministries of Labour, especially if provided with labour attachés in the diplomatic corps, marks an advance not only in domestic politics but in the relation of peoples. It is obviously more important to know the trade unions abroad than the " society " which no longer controls politics or the number of a nation's rifles ; and it is perhaps equally obvious that the older diplomacy is not well fitted for understanding or promoting the contact of the nine-tenths of every nation who are the manual workers.[1]

One detail in regard to method has received undue attention—the secrecy of diplomatic dealings. Obviously diplomatic action should be the conscious act of the whole people ; and the people should know to what they are committed, for what purpose and on what conditions. There should be greater publicity than there is now, both for the general enlightenment of the public and for the prevention of the activities of sinister influences. But everyone knows that, first, an agent must be trusted and cannot at every moment be examined or put on trial ; and, secondly, negotiations in process must be regarded as confidential. There is nothing disgraceful in being polite : nor is the best conversation carried on at the top of one's voice : nor again are confidences always scandalous.[2] It is true, however, that even as a diplomatic method the secret and the confidential have been greatly over-valued by officials : and it should be remembered that in practice there is often little difference between keeping a secret and practising deceit and fraud. Further the experience of the war has shown the need of communicating with foreign peoples as well as their governments. Official propaganda, it is true, especially in war, which is essentially the practice of fraud, obstructs rather than promotes international goodwill ; but the implied method of approaching a foreign people through open statements in the press or elsewhere may be susceptible of a useful development.

The non-diplomatic branch of the foreign services, the Consular, has different purposes and different methods. It is more closely connected with law, trade and the contact of individuals rather than states. The Consular official performs marriage ceremonies, rescues stranded nationals, gives information to traders and is generally in closer contact with foreign peoples in smaller towns. The Con-

---

[1] This of course is not a complete account of the contact of modern states. Ministers of Education, Health, and even Justice and Police now have their foreign contacts.

[2] This does not justify secret *treaties*. Binding agreements are, of course, in a different category from negotiations, *cf.* below, p. 129.

sular service verges on the diplomatic in the near East; and in such countries, for example, as Albania the Consulates of Austria, Russia, Italy and Great Britain were the scenes of diplomatic controversy for the control of the Balkan situation by one or other of the Great Powers.[1] On the other hand, the Consular service may perform a genuine international function by reports on the situation abroad. For example, after the report on the Putumayo atrocities and the conclusions of a select Committee of the British House of Commons, a circular letter was issued by the British Foreign Secretary instructing consular officers to report on labour conditions in their districts, especially where the companies operating were wholly or partly controlled by British subjects. This is connected with the general consular instructions to report on slavery: but the meaning is extended and there is evidence here of a much larger than the old view of moral responsibility and the function of government.[2]

It is usual to suppose that a Consular, as opposed to a Diplomatic, official should promote trade; and the Royal Commission on the Civil Service reports that "in some quarters we have noticed an impression that a Consular Officer should perform the duties of a commercial traveller and secure sales for the products of particular manufacturers or contracts or concessions for particular firms. But consuls are not qualified to perform services of this kind, and it is undesirable in the general interests of this country that they should attempt to perform them. The Consular Service like the Diplomatic Service exists for the benefit of the community as a whole, and the influence and efficiency of either service are impaired when it becomes identified with the interests of individual traders or concessionaires."[3] Here is a political principle of the first importance. It affects the whole conception of the state and it implies that the state is by no means an economic unit, that it does not exist for trade, nor for producers, nor for consumers; but for justice and liberty.

Apart from the everyday communication between governments through the diplomatic system, there is a special apparatus of conferences and congresses which result in

[1] *cf.* M. E. Durham, "High Albania," p. 10 and *passim*.
[2] Report of Committee, Parliamentary papers No. 509 (Session 1912,13), Circular of December 15, 1913.
[3] Cd. 7748, Sect. 13.

conventions, treaties or agreements. The most famous conferences and treaties have been connected with the close of great wars : but in some cases the governments have been able to consider a problem before it had led to actual warfare.

At the close of wars, congresses generally are meetings of the belligerents, but since no war is quite confined in its effects to the belligerents there has been a tendency to invite or allow the presence of neutrals. At the Congress of Vienna there were 216 representatives of separate governments, although there were only eight parties to the Treaty of Paris (May 30, 1814) which the Congress was to consider. All congresses at the end of wars tend to be dominated by war passions and war is essentially a confession of political bankruptcy in international affairs.

Conferences not for the ending of wars mark an advance. In the nineteenth century there were several for the purpose of arranging policy in regard to possible subjects of dispute. Conferences with regard to Balkan affairs developed into the so-called Concert of Europe : and the conferences in regard to Africa (Berlin, 1885 ; Brussels, 1890) developed a primitive kind of colonial internationalism.[1] The Conference held at the Foreign Office in London in 1913 at the end of the first Balkan War was an example of a combination of both principles, the making of a peace and the world-conference in view of future difficulties ; but the Treaty then signed (May 30) did not prevent a return to war and a new Treaty of the belligerents had to be signed at Bukarest (July 30), the whole situation being the descent to the great downfall of August, 1914. The most important conferences, however, for our present purpose were those held at the Hague in 1899 and 1907 to which reference is made below.

In regard to treaties the most important fact is the number of treaties which are normally effective. The violation of treaties by Italy in 1911 and Germany in 1914 has caused a popular misunderstanding as to the treaty-system : but the vast majority of treaties are faithfully maintained and the credit-system involved in the confidence of the parties is really the basis for the whole of international dealings.

[1] For details see Rose, " Development of the European Nations," and for a discussion of some principles involved, see my " Morality of Nations."

DIPLOMACY

There are various kinds of agreement. A treaty is a specially solemn agreement and is ratified when the head of a state solemnly declares that he accepts its provisions. That declaration is made public, after an exchange of ratifications, by proclamation. A less formal agreement is called a Convention:[1] and a new form of Convention is a Declaration, as for example that of Paris (1856) on blockade, etc., and that of London (1909) in regard to naval warfare.[2] Such a Declaration is in fact an international agreement as to principles. There is also a form technically known as an Agreement, as for example that between Great Britain and Japan in regard to China and Korea (January 30, 1902): and there is the less formal "Arrangement" as, for example, those which govern the use of trade marks. All these involve formal and carefully considered, signed documents; but a less formal record more speedily negotiated is sometimes used, especially as a preliminary or as an addendum to formal treaties, and it is called a Protocol.[3] The names are historic and they are valuable indications of the stages through which international politics has passed.

The treaty system is endangered by one of the worst elements in the diplomatic tradition, the existence of secret arrangements between governments. The practice of making secret agreements during a war must be distinguished from secrecy in times of peace, unless indeed Treitschke is right and peace is only "veiled war." War is in essence fraud as well as force and a government committed to war is hardly able to avoid spying, deceit, lies and secret treaties. This may be the explanation of the several secret arrangements and treaties entered into by both sides in the recent great war:[4] but there is evidence that attempts at separate understandings were entered into even as between belligerents.[5]

[1] The Geneva Conventions, 1864 and 1906, on the Red Cross, due to the humane feelings of M. Dunant, a Swiss citizen, is perhaps less controversial but not less formal than a treaty.

[2] Texts of Declarations, Conventions, etc., are given in Higgins, "The Hague Peace Conferences," etc.

[3] A *Protocole de Compromis* or a *Compromis* is an agreement to submit a case to enquiry.

[4] "Texts of the Secret Treaties," ed. by Seymour Cocks. Italian-French Treaty described, *International Review*, February, 1919. *cf.* also the Sykes-Picot Agreement (*Manchester Guardian*, January 8, 1920), and the Italian Agreement (*id.*, January 9).

[5] " Efforts towards the conclusion of a separate peace and an alliance between Germany, Russia and Japan were made by the

Much more corrosive of international confidence is the tendency to underhand dealings in times of peace, embodied in secret agreements. That such exist has been indicated by undesigned revelations. Thus while Italy renewed her alliance with Germany in 1902 she entered into a secret treaty with France at the same time, details of which were given only in December, 1918. Again the declaration as to the status of Egypt and Morocco made by France and Great Britain in 1904 gave the world to understand that no change was contemplated: but secret articles existed, which were unknown to the public until revealed without authority in 1911; and these articles provide for "modifying the policy in respect to Egypt or Morocco."[1] Naturally little is known of the extent of the practice; but the fact that little is known makes the public suspicion all the greater; and obviously the practice corrodes the whole of the credit on which the normal intercourse of governments is based. The peoples are committed to action of the danger of which they have not even been warned.

The whole diplomatic system, Foreign Offices, ambassadors, consuls, conferences and their products, treaties, is dominated by the antique conception that a common interest will be attained most easily by a conflict of opposing interests. This is the hypothesis of foreign as contrasted with international policy: but many members of the Foreign services in many countries have thought and acted internationally. It is true that some of the interests of a nation are opposed to some of the interests of other nations and in these cases adjustment and compromise are the only practical methods for policy, since the evidence does not give any indication of how practically to reduce all contending interests to the terms of a common interest.

Diplomacy, however, is often compelled by the nature of the subject to be dealt with to think and act internationally, and instances have been given above of such cases in reference to the Balkan Wars and the partition of Africa. Various international Commissions also have been set up

German Government in March, 1916, by the German ambassador in Stockholm, through the Japanese ambassador," *Far Eastern Review*, quoted in *International Review*, November, 1919.

[1] *See* above, p. 73. The secret articles can be found in Barclay's "Turco-Italian War," p. 184, Appendix III. The draft of a secret treaty of October, 1918, between Japan and Germany for the "settlement" of Russia was published in the *International Review*, November, 1919.

within the diplomatic system for dealing with boundaries and other such subjects : but perhaps the best instance of the need for international diplomacy is to be found in the treatment of canals, straits and rivers traversing many countries. Permanent Commissions are referred to below,[1] but diplomacy of an international character may be found in the case of the Dardanelles and Bosphorus, Suez and Panama. The Bosphorus controversy has been largely concerned with the passage of ships of war. The Treaty of Paris, 1856, closed the straits to warships, but this restriction on her power was repudiated by Russia in 1870. The Treaty of London, 1891, allowed Turkey to close the straits to warships and this continued to be the accepted international rule when the great war began. The whole question in fact turns on the danger of war and its effects on the commerce of the world.[2] The Suez Canal was opened in 1869 and was "neutralised" after much controversy by a Convention of 1888 signed by six Great Powers of Europe, Turkey, Spain and the Netherlands ; but Great Britain made a reservation in reference to her control in Egypt and the position of the Canal is hardly international at present.

The Panama Canal was opened in 1914. Its use is largely governed by the Hay-Pauncefote Treaties of 1900 and 1901 by which Great Britain withdrew all claims and left the canal to the United States, on conditions similar to those governing the Suez Canal. Treaties of 1902 and 1903 give equal commercial use of the Panama Canal to ships of all flags, and the specially low rates for United States ships, allowed by an Act of 1912, were abrogated by an Act of 1914. The canal has been fortified by the United States. In all these cases the freedom to merchant ships and even to warships in time of peace is granted : but the danger of war creates apparently insuperable difficulties and obviously no international agreement can fully envisage the position of such important waterways in a future war.

The truth is that diplomacy, which deals traditionally

---

[1] p. 147.
[2] Exactions in time of peace are not usual now ; but were once practised. The passage to the Baltic was only freed from exactions by Denmark by the Treaty of Copenhagen, 1857. For the Bosphorus see Woolf, " Future of Constantinople," and Phillipson and Buxton, " Bosphorus and the Dardanelles " (1917), especially the general chapter on waterways.

with "foreign" policy, cannot effectively deal with international policy so long as the danger of war overshadows the whole international situation. War does, in fact, dominate the thought of the majority of those who are concerned with the contact between the governments of the world.

The reason for this is, in the main, that states in international politics are treated and act in accordance with their title as "Powers." They are, that is to say, organised groups of a certain wealth and military efficiency. Their different degrees of civilisation or excellence of government are of little importance in foreign affairs. What matters is their income and their armed forces. Thus it matters very little that Denmark is more highly developed than Italy: for Italy is wealthier and has a larger army and navy. The opinion or desires of the representative of Italy has greater weight than that of others, not because his people are more highly educated, better judges of fact, or better governed, but because they can supply more cash and more man-power. Armies and navies are, therefore, of extreme importance in foreign policy and in diplomacy. They are the facts which give point to the desires of diplomats or of peoples: and the reflection of this is to be seen in the information available as to foreign states, for the reference books give many details as to naval and military affairs but very little as to natural resources and none at all as to the organisation of labour or employers in the different countries.[1] Armaments in general are defended on the ground of natural selection and the utility of force in discovering which nation "ought" to prevail: but these arguments are like those which would give to the strong individual all rights against the weak. They can only be believed by those who imagine a nation to be some mysterious entity, not men, women and children.[2]

Armaments create a problem but they are very commonly supposed to be the solution of a problem. They are an excellent instance of political ineptitude since the problem they solve is simple by comparison to the problem they create. Armaments are said on every hand to be kept

[1] The *Almanach de Gotha* and the *Statesman's Year Book* indicate the prevailing preoccupation with force and wealth.

[2] *cf.* Spencer Wilkinson, "Government and the War," and A. T. Mahan, "Armaments and Arbitration," for political nonsense.

for the sake of peace, since all armaments are for defence. They solve, therefore, the problem of how we are to be preserved from any persons who may want to govern us against our will or to interfere with our interests. But they create the problem of increasing costs, for when a nation has begun to arm for defence only, there is no point at which it can logically stop. The chief European states spent about £105,719,000 in 1870 on armaments and about £208,877,000 in 1898. The expenditure had almost been doubled in those twenty-eight years; but they were inexpensive years as compared with to-day. There was an increasing expenditure as the nations neared self-defence in August 1914:[1] and now unfortunately it is quite impossible to calculate the bankruptcy of the final effort. In 1914-15 the British war credits amounted to £362,000,000: and in 1918-19 (March 4th) they amounted to £3,000,000,000. This, however, takes no account of the absorption of the whole engineering trade of the civilised world in the making of munitions, the waste of brains, energy and material in devising force to counteract force and the shutting down of all those activities which are usually connected with civilisation.

If this is the only method of avoiding foreign aggression it seems likely to destroy everything which might be worth defending: and if diplomacy can devise no better system it is proved incompetent, still more so if it needs this system for securing small territories and possible prestige or ready cash. It is not true, however, that armaments are only for defence against aggression; for, in the first place, it is agreed that the best defence is an offensive and therefore there is no distinguishing aggression from defence; and, secondly, armaments exist largely from habit and the atavistic tastes of certain persons in every state. Habit makes the gentleman of to-day model himself on the knight of the middle ages,

[1] Expenditure on Armaments.

	Military.		Naval.	
	1905-6.	1912-13.	1905-6.	1912-13.
Great Britain	28,850,000	28,071,000	33,151,841	48,809,300
France	27,393,379	39,328,975	12,667,856	19,072,945
Russia	39,048,390	58,606,428	12,392,684	17,681,213
Italy	11,281,828	17,260,902	5,040,000	10,054,505
Austria	12,874,840	17,739,814	1,838,975	7,867,644
Germany	35,259,584	43,389,775	11,300,000	22,215,000

it makes arms appear the true profession of kings and the highest service of the state, it makes state functions appear primarily as military displays. Some groups, for example in Arabia and in Prussia, are completely dominated by the habit of arms.

The most interesting problem of armaments however is connected with what is called private enterprise. The great armament firms, Armstrongs, Schneiders, Krupps and their fellows, have been unjustly abused by some because they sought profits from the killing and maiming of men and the destruction of civilised life : and yet the real trouble is not that they sought the profits but that the peoples of the world are willing and eager to pay the profits. The fundamental fact is that the demand for armaments is so great and so varied that the governments have not been able to supply it themselves : and since it has been shown in the recent war that the popular appetite for munitions of war may absorb the energies of almost the whole of a nation's industries, it is evident that, short of state-socialism, there is still likely to be some private enterprise in supplying civilisation with enough rope to hang itself.

The armaments trade in the United Kingdom has been before the war chiefly in the hands of three great combines—Sir G. Armstrong, Whitworth and Co., Vickers, Ltd., and Cammell Laird, John Brown and Co. ; but the most recent arrangements or amalgamations are not yet generally known. Armstrongs present (1919) capital is £9,512,500. Besides the great works at Elswick and the Walker shipyard, Armstrongs control the Armstrong-Pozzuoli Co., with works on the bay of Naples and the Ansaldo-Armstrong Co. of Genoa, which built warships both for Italy and for Turkey, thus appearing without prejudice in the Turco-Italian war. Armstrongs combine with Vickers to supply half the capital of armament works at Muroran in Japan. Armstrongs, Vickers and John Brown's combine to control the Hispana works at Ferrol in Spain. By means of inter-locking directorates Armstrongs have part control of the Whitehead Torpedo Works (Weymouth) Ltd., directors of which before the war had control of the Whitehead torpedo works at Fiume where the Austrian torpedoes were produced which were useful against British ships in the late war. Among the directors of Armstrongs many instances may

DIPLOMACY

be found of close connection with state officials; for example, Rear-Admiral Sir C. L. Ottley, formerly naval attaché in U.S.A., Japan, Italy, Russia and France, Director of Naval Intelligence 1905 to 1907 and later Secretary to the Committee of Imperial Defence.[1]

Vickers, Ltd., has capital of £7,400,000 in ordinary shares, £1,250,000 preference and about £2,000,000 debentures. In 1902 it took over half the shares of W. Beardmore and Co., Ltd. It controls the Vickers-Terni Co., of Genoa. It has now began the supply of aeroplanes to China as well as the setting up of repair shops there.[2] One of the directors is Sir Vincent Caillard, who was financial representative of England, Holland and Belgium in Constantinople from 1883 to 1898.

Cammell Laird and Co., a combine formed in 1903, entered in 1905 into a working arrangement with John Brown and Co. of Sheffield and the Fairfield Shipbuilding and Engineering Co. of Glasgow. By inter-locking directorates and holdings, the combine controls many apparently independent firms.

Neither the size of the firms nor their connection with state officials is remarkable considering the public appetite for armaments and the fact that the State is the chief " consumer " There is, of course, nothing astonishing in the profits earned nor in the movement towards combination, both of which can be found in other industries. What is important for international politics is that there are strong groups which derive gain from war and the threat of war; and that part of the gain is derived from sales of war material to foreign nations. Thus the export of war vessels from the United Kingdom in 1913 was valued at £2,617,000 and the export of arms, ammunitions and military stores for 1913 was valued at £2,426,216, of which goods valued at £18,070 went to Germany, £10,883 to Turkey and £23,708 to Austria.[3] In 1914 the export of the same kinds of material amounted to £3,005,464 of which £50,656 worth went to Turkey: and yet Great Britain was at war with Germany and Austria by August 1914 and with Turkey by November 1914.

The sale of war material is, of course, reciprocal; for

---

[1] It is indicated in the *Times*, October 11, 1919, that India is to be a new field for armament firms.

[2] *Times*, October 3, 1919. *See* above, p. 70.

[3] Cd. 9127 (1918).

Great Britain imported arms and ammunition from Germany to the following amounts:—

Year	1909.	1910.	1911.	1912.	1913.
Value	£79,138	£85,174	£112,898	£138,788	£150,253

It will also be remembered that Great Britain bought eighteen batteries of field artillery from the Rheinische Metalwaarenfabrik in 1901.

The supply of small wars is a source of gain to the armaments industry, which, in every country, is willing to supply both sides while its own country remains neutral. The Balkan Wars of 1912, 1913, were fought almost entirely with armaments and munitions supplied by the more civilised nations. Thus the export of war material from the United Kingdom to *both sides* in the war may be seen from these figures:—

Export of Arms, etc.	1909. £	1910. £	1911. £	1912. £	1913. £
To Turkey	21,696	94,677	86,619	8,778	10,883
To Serbia	336	12,094	10,972	1,740	—
To Greece	4,535	24,519	40,982	43,905	83,165

Obviously other sources of supply were available; and some of these other sources can be traced in the French and German statistics of export.[1] France exported goods of the following values in 1912 (values in pounds sterling approximately):

	To Turkey.	To Greece.
Guns	48,546	3,565
Small Arms Ammunition	47,104	23,040
Projectiles	98,576	7,936

In the same year France exported projectiles to Bulgaria valued at £53,584: and guns to Great Britain valued at £62,651. In 1913 France continued to arm Turkey, exporting to her guns worth £108,996: so that the guns of Gallipoli may well have been made in France.

[1] "Tableau générale de Com. et Nav.," Vol. I, p. 668, and the German Trade Statistics.

Germany also was useful in 1912, supplying small arms ammunition to Turkey worth £395,300, and to the enemies of Turkey, Bulgaria and Greece, ammunition worth £39,750 and £21,850 respectively. After all the Schneider and the Krupp shareholders have to live as well as the shareholders in Vickers and Armstrongs.

From 1856 to 1859 Krupps was arming the Khedive of Egypt ; in 1866 Krupps rearmed the whole Belgian field artillery and supplied new model guns to Russia. After the establishment of the German Empire in 1871 the Imperial Government entered into close relations with Krupps, which was engaged to rearm the German field artillery by July 1, 1875.[1] The business was a family affair until 1903 when it became a company with capital of £9,000,000 one of the largest shareholders being the late Kaiser, Wilhelm II, a personal friend of the Krupp who died in 1902, whose heiress married in 1906, Baron Krupp von Bohlen, a diplomatist who had served in the German Legations at Pekin, Washington and the Vatican.[2] In 1907 the German Government granted a loan of £2,500,000 for enlarging the Essen works, in order to enable Krupps to carry out larger contracts. In October 1912 Liebknecht revealed that Krupps had secret information as to contracts and competitors from the German War Office and two directors of Krupps were tried and " punished."

The situation in other industrialised nations is not essentially different. In France, Schneider and Co., the St. Chamond Steel Co. and the Compagnie des Forges, in the United States the Bethlehem Steel Co. and the Carnegie Co. depend on government orders and naturally have close relations with their governments.

Certain difficulties sometimes arise from such a situation. In the way of trade government officials may become confused, as for example in the case of the Japanese naval officials in the years immediately preceding the war. Large sums were received from armament firms by certain officials on condition that contracts should be given to those firms ; but the mere fact of bribery is

---

[1] In 1901 Krupps supplied machine guns to the Indian Government, *cf.* H. R. Murray, " Krupps."

[2] The University of Bonn in 1915 presented the Baron with a Ph.D. in honour of his great gun which laid low Namur, and of his submarines.

not important here.[1] What is important is that if armament contracts can be increased, if any government can be induced to increase its army and navy, many other governments necessarily increase theirs : rivalry becomes more acute and more unendurable and war is sensibly nearer. It is felt by many that this should not be caused by a mere desire for profits on the part of the firms which practise bribery.

Again, there is the governmental " scare." For armament firms desiring orders nothing is better than fear of foreign expansion in armaments : for this trade is peculiar in its desire for the foreigner to increase his own products. In 1909 for example Mr. Mulliner of the Coventry Ordnance Works informed the British Government of excessive shipbuilding by Germany : which produced orders in Great Britain, although the news was unfortunately found to be untrue.[2]

Internationalism of another kind is to be seen in the world-wide connections of the great armament firms : but internationalism was even more clearly embodied in the Harvey United Steel Co., a combine uniting Krupps, the Dillengen Co. (Bavaria), Vickers, Armstrong, John Brown and Co., Cammell Laird, Schneider (Creusot), Vickers-Terni and Ansaldo-Armstrong (for Italy) and the Bethlehem Steel Co. (U.S.A.) This combine was for the control of certain patents for armour-plate and is now dissolved : it is, however, symptomatic of the brotherhood of arms, and obviously nothing but joint action on the part of governments can control the dangerous tendencies to combination in this most important trade. The persons concerned are not villains. Their moral and political conceptions are those of the majority of men to-day, but they are nevertheless obsolete.

It is recognised that the extension of the trade in armaments may cause difficulties at least when the smaller governments or the uncivilised peoples begin to buy.

The trade in arms was regulated by the Brussels Con-

[1] The facts and documents are to be found in the *Japan Chronicle* of the early months of 1914. Siemens-Schuckert at Tokio gave bribes for contracts for electrical apparatus ; but the controllers of the firm in Germany declared that the bribery was without their sanction. Japanese Admirals were put on trial in Japan, one being charged with receiving £35,270 in 1911, 1912, from contractors, including two well-known British shipbuilding firms.

[2] Perris, " War Traders," p. 114 *seq*.

vention of 1890 : but a new Convention was signed on September 10, 1919, which had in view " the accumulation in various parts of the world of considerable quantities of arms and munitions of war, the dispersal of which would constitute a danger to peace and public order."[1] The export of arms is forbidden except under licence ; and special mention is made of Africa (except Algeria, Libya and South Africa), Transcaucasia, Persia, Arabia, etc., but here again licences may be given. Provision is made for powers of a naval patrol especially over " native " vessels : and this is obviously a problem for effective administration rather than formal agreement. The control of the trade in arms entirely depends upon the character of the administration of the several states and the policy actually followed in granting licences. This is good as far as it goes ; but it does not solve the difficulty of the greater offenders. The great states of the world are the chief buyers of arms and they are uncontrolled. The problem of increasing expenditure on armaments has, however, been recognised by all governments and it is referred to in the Covenant of the League of Nations.

Certain general principles are believed to govern the action of governments in foreign politics, and of these there are two which are most commonly practised : one is the support of a particular form of government abroad, the other is the Balance of Power. It was believed during the war that there was a specifically German policy which implied (1) as an aim, the military and economic domination of one group of states or one form of government over all others, and (2) as a means, the use of force and fraud. That these principles do in fact underlie the policy of various governments cannot be doubted. But it is doubtful whether they are specifically German or Prussian, since they can be found in ancient history in the policy of England, France, Spain and other countries : and if it were not impolite, traces could be found of the same policy in the actions of most existing governments. What is more important is the less extreme version of this older principle. For example, the Allies have supported Koltchak, Denikin, and in Hungary, Admiral Horthy,[2] not as " reactionaries "

[1] Cmd. 414, Treaty Series, No. 12 (1919).
[2] For a judgment of the Allies' action and its effect on neighbouring peoples see *Arbeiter-Zeitung*, November 18, 1919. It is there said that Horthy stands for Hungarian feudalism.

but as representatives of "democratic government." This implies the pathetic belief that the Government of England, especially in Ireland and India, or of France in Dahomey or Italy in Libya is democratic.[1] But the mere word should not confuse us. The point is that there is a kind of government which is familiar; and the principle of policy seems to be that that kind or something like it must be established. This involves not, of course, the domination of one nationality over all others, but the domination of one social class over all others. And, as for the means—any means appear to be acceptable in foreign politics. Such a policy cannot be called unpopular; because the arrangement of social and political life on the principle of class domination appears to be enthusiastically welcomed by great numbers even of those who suffer from this domination. The Hungarian peasant, for example, prefers his local lords to the administration of the town proletariat and perhaps the Russian peasant would prefer the corrupt aristocracy to the city intellectuals as rulers. Even when class domination is not welcomed, it is accepted as natural by the great majority; and this acquiescence in what is customary has been dignified with the name of the "General Will." Thus easily is it shown how government actually depends upon the consent of the governed and how truly this or that form of government is democratic.

The second great principle of foreign policy is the Balance of Power, which implies the use of the simplest instrument of diplomacy—force and the threat of force. The origin of the conception of the Balance is well known. When first the unity of Europe, based upon the culture and religion of the Middle Ages, was dissolved, the atomic sovereign states of the Renaissance were found to be of different military power and in continually changing relations. It was felt by the diplomatists of the day that some stability could be introduced and some security for the weak as

[1] Nothing will be more amusing to the cynical historian of the future than the indignation of the governing class in the United States, which really believes in "democracy," against any unfamiliar form even of majority rule. The idea that anything may be wrong in the government of the United States is amusingly refuted by the Federal Court in the case of the condemnation of youthful critics to twenty years imprisonment in the year 1919. See the case of Abrams v. U.S.A. Judgments published in *New Republic*, November 26, 1919.

DIPLOMACY

against the strong, by balancing the forces, so that a strong government might be less likely to rush into war. The Balance of Power was certainly conceived at first as a policy for avoiding war; and it is still so conceived by the simple-minded or the very old. The Balance may possibly defer war in some cases since no government would move towards war unless it felt that its force was likely to overbalance the force of its opponents: but the natural and inevitable result of the principle has been the gradual accumulation of force by states or groups of states whose governments thought their interests to be opposed to those of another group; and this accumulation inevitably results in precipitating immense wars when wars do come. Every day, therefore, by which the Balance of Power puts off a war makes a great war more inevitable and, since the principle of the Balance is again embodied in the Treaty of Versailles, a more devastating war than that of 1914–1918 is absolutely inevitable so long as the policy of the Balance of Power dominates the relation between states.[1]

On the hypothesis that a great war is inevitable as soon as the peoples have somewhat forgotten the last, it is reasonable that preparations should be made and therefore that money should be expended increasingly on armaments and youth more and more absorbed in unproductive military training. These preparations make the great war still more inevitable and so by an ever increasing momentum the human race moves in the precarious equipoise of the Balance of Power towards its attainment of the status and the policy of the anthropoid apes. It is a distant fate, which has no terrors for the inhabitant of the drawing-room or the slum kitchen: but meantime the policy of the Balance reduces every day the available amount of leisure

[1] Thus Hanotaux, after dismissing President Wilson's principles (p. 234), and dealing with the League on one page (p. 336), says: "Tout systeme d'alliance ser attaché à la vieille politique, à cette politique de l'equilibre tant raillée. Du moins ici, le terrain est solide": discounting the earthquake of 1914–1918. Again, "La France doit jouer, dans les affaires di l'Europe continentale un role prépondérante," discounting the Balance ("Le Traité de Versailles," p. 343, published September, 1919.) *cf.* French Official Report, 1918, on "l'Alliance Franco-Russe." The French Minister at Petersburg, August 24, 1890, writes to M. Ribot of the "defaut de notre constitution qui a privé notre politique des avantages du sécret." The full text of military conventions against the Triple Alliance is given. The object was to "safeguard the equilibrium of European forces."

and consumable commodities ; it degrades the machinery of government and obstructs the growth of individual freedom ; and all this is not desired by the majority of men although they are easily persuaded that it is inevitable.

In view of this situation, it may well be doubted whether the Balance of Power is a solution of a problem and not rather the creation of new problems : but the alternative to the Balance is referred to below and here it is enough to have pointed out some of the absurdities upon which the conception of the Balance rests.

CHAPTER VII

OFFICIAL INTERNATIONAL ORGANISATION

FOREIGN policy is, as indicated above, the pursuit of a separate interest usually conceived as opposed to that of other governments or peoples. International policy is the pursuit of an interest conceived to be common to all peoples. Diplomacy contains examples of both kinds of policy: and although the more primitive conceptions and practices have survived with a certain virulence in the dealings between governments, a new system has been developing. International Law, world conferences of governments, and organisation for joint or agreed action between governments—all contribute evidence of the existence and increasing importance of the practice of international politics.

It has been often noted in reference to treaties and agreements that there is nothing in the sphere of international politics exactly corresponding to law and legislation in domestic politics: for if treaties are International Law, they are in fact agreements and not " commands of a superior," while their sanction is not police force but, if it may be called a sanction, public opinion. The question whether International Law is really law is entirely and absolutely futile: but apart from the mere question of words, it is questionable whether the lawyer's traditional view of domestic legislation is not mistaken. Legislation may perhaps not be the command of a superior and law may not be a command in any sense except so far as the form—" Thou shalt not " is traditional. The idea of a superior has caused many unnecessary puzzles as to self government and " myself," in one sense, commanding " myself " in another sense—all which appears to be primitive metaphysics. The truth is that even domestic law is in essence an agreement between equals in regard to principles which govern their relationship: and law is a general statement, not a command, still less a negative command.[1] But if this is true, then International Law is real law and indeed more truly law than the Acts of the Sovereign in domestic affairs : and it has its two parts in regard to the relation of groups (states, etc., i.e. public law) and in regard to the relation of individuals (nationality, domicile, etc., i.e. private law).

The relation of states, which are the " subjects " of international law, is based upon the conception of sovereignty : and sovereignty in this sense implies complete independence in external relations.[2] It has, however, been necessary to recognise what is called part-sovereign states, and the distinction between Great Powers and other states makes a difference to the dealings of governments. Indeed it is obvious that frontiers do not limit the legitimate activities of governments and that the circumstances in one state may seriously affect the situation in all others : therefore *intervention* has in fact often occurred,[3] and the policy of non-intervention is only a protest against interference with changes of government or civil wars. This is an instance of the need for developing international principles of politics in place of a mere conflict of foreign policies and state rights. In the normal activities of governments, however, such issues do not arise : sovereign rights are accepted internationally in regard to defined territories (the high seas are without any sovereign) and in regard to natural-born or naturalised subjects. The intercourse of states in diplomacy has already been described.

All international dealings are overshadowed by the institution called war, and therefore a great part of formulated custom in International Law deals with war. It was regarded as legal, although undesirable, by the first

[1] This theory is argued more fully in my " Morality of Nations."
[2] Internal (political) sovereignty is ultimate authority over constituents of a state : " legal " sovereignty is the distinguishing mark of the source of law in practice. Internal sovereignty has been sometimes taken to mean absolute and unlimited authority ; but in this sense the state cannot possibly be " sovereign " without the destruction of civilised life. External sovereignty has been taken to mean, not merely " independence," but absolute and unlimited rights without any *moral* responsibility for acts ; but in this sense of sovereignty again the state would be the most obnoxious of institutions. *cf*. Laski, " Problem of Sovereignty " and " Authority in the Modern State."
[3] Intervention of European Powers in 1860 in Turkish massacres in Lebanon, of European Powers in China, 1900, of U.S.A. in Cuba, 1898 and 1906.

International jurists for the armed bands of one state to slaughter all subjects of the other state with which they were at war : but now limitations to the use of force are commonly practised. The wounded are not commonly slaughtered, prisoners are usually fed and clothed, and a vague distinction is admitted between combatants and non-combatants. Attempts are usually made to distinguish also between state property and private property, since the conception survives that war is a relation of states rather than of citizens of the states. This, however, originates in the old distinction between the people and their government and is irreconcilable with the conception that the state is in some sense the people, who are responsible for the acts of their agents, the government. Similar difficulties arise out of the practices connected with neutrality : for the old idea that a blockade, for example, could injure belligerents without seriously affecting neutrals is obviously false in the modern world. All wars are international in their effects : and therefore the position of non-belligerents will have to be reconsidered. Enough, however, has been said to indicate the province of international rules in regard to the contact of peoples organised as states under governments. The organisation of peace has hardly begun to attract the attention or to govern the policies of governments; for most of their efforts, when they have risen to any international effort at all, have been devoted to the attempt to moderate the excesses of that barbaric anarchy known as war.

The organisation of peace, however, began with the many arbitration treaties of the nineteenth century; and the practice of arbitration was successful enough to prove that governments could use political intelligence instead of force in international affairs. The next step was the creation of an international tribunal which did in fact give decisions which were accepted by the parties. Both these advances were connected with the Hague Conference.

The international Conferences and Conventions with limited objects lead up to the two great "Peace" Conferences at The Hague in 1899 and 1907.[1] The first was summoned, after a circular letter of the Tsar, by the Dutch Government, and the Tsar's original intention was that a limitation of armaments should be discussed. This,

[1] cf. Higgins, "The Hague Peace Conferences," etc. T. J. Lawrence, "International Problems and the Hague."

however, was regarded as presenting too many difficulties. At the first Conference twenty-six states were represented:[1] the results were three conventions (1) for the pacific settlement of international disputes, (2) regarding the laws of war on land, (3) application of the Geneva Convention to sea warfare. There were also three declarations made, (1) against explosives from balloons, (2) against gas shells, and (3) against explosive bullets. A pious resolution was added that the restriction of expenditure on armaments is "desirable." When the Conventions had been agreed, war followed, first between Great Britain and the South African republics and next between Russia and Japan. A Court of Arbitration, however, had been established which tried four important cases involving the danger of war.

The initiative in calling the second Conference was taken by President Roosevelt, but the actual invitation came from the Tsar. Forty-four states were represented.[2] The second Conference amended the Convention of the first in regard to the pacific settlement of disputes, provided for arbitration (as against force) for recovery of debts (Drago doctrine) : the other eleven Conventions all relate to the customs of war and are attempts to restrict the use of force. The presence of large numbers of small states all claiming equality with the Great Powers led to the hopeless method of deciding on a recommendation only if unanimity could be secured. There was also an inordinate length and frequency of speeches, and it was obvious that one of the most important items in an international conference should be definite rules of procedure. As for the Conventions, it is significant that the so-called "Peace" Conferences dealt chiefly with the customs of *war* : and this is unfortunately still the tendency in International Law. The only positive contribution to international political life was the Convention (of 97 articles) dealing with "Good Offices" and "Mediation" (the use of third states as mediators), Commissions of Inquiry,[3] Arbitration and the Permanent

---

[1] No South or Central American states were represented.

[2] Korea was excluded because Japan asserted its entire control of the foreign policy of that country. *cf.* Higgins, *op. cit.*, pp. 35, 56.

[3] Used in regard to the Dogger Bank incident, October 21st, 1904. The Commission met on December 22 and gave its award on February 26, 1905. It is possible also to say that the Convention against the use of force for collecting debts was an advance : but several states did not sign.

OFFICIAL INTERNATIONAL ORGANISATION 147

Court at The Hague. The whole situation, however, has been changed by the great war and the Covenant of the League of Nations which is dealt with below.

Diplomacy and periodical Conferences have not proved sufficient for international needs, even in the opinions of the governments, before the war ; and therefore many international organisations were formed for administrative action on an international scale. The following are the chief public international unions with administrative offices which were in existence before the war :[1]

A.—Communications : Universal Postal Union (1874), Telegraphic Union, Radiotelegraphic Union, Railway Freight Transportation Bureau (1890).

B.—Information : The International Institute of Agriculture (1905), International Geodetic Association, International Seismological Union, International Bureau of Police, International Metric Union (1875), International Office of Public Health (1907), Pan-American Sanitary Union.

C.—Trade and Commerce : Office of Trade Marks, Office of Copyright.

D.—Undefined : Pan-American Union, Central American Union.

There are also permanent international Commissions for specific purposes, either regulating special districts, as in the case of the Danube Commission, the Congo Commission, the Suez Canal Commission, etc., or for commodities, as the Sugar Commission and the Opium Commission. Finally, various conferences have led to the unification of the laws and the assimilation of the administration in many states, as in the case of the Latin Monetary Union, the White Slave Traffic, the Automobile Conference, Submarine Cables and Commercial Statistics.

The difference between foreign policy and international policy may be understood by reference to the traffic in opium. It was at one time conceived to be a British interest to sell opium from India to the Chinese : and Great Britain went to war with China in 1840 to compel her to accept a trade which was regarded by the more enlightened Chinese as corrupting to the people of China.[2] This was

[1] L. S. Woolf, " International Government," p. 102. This book gives full details of the history of international offices and agreements.

[2] Other issues also were involved, and obviously the Chinese policy of exclusion was partly to blame.

foreign policy : but Great Britain adopted an international policy in an agreement of 1911 to diminish the export of Indian opium in proportion as the production in China decreased ; and an international Convention for the control of the opium trade was signed in 1912.[1] In 1917, China was declared free of opium and Indian import ceased ; but in the civil war the growth of opium began again in 1918 in China. Local military governors preferred to tax opium rather than suppress it.

Conventions are inadequate without a genuine international policy affecting domestic legislation in the states concerned. The defect has not been altogether in China. The export of morphia from Great Britain to Japan greatly increased during the war, from 30,000 ounces a year to 600,000 in 1917. Licences for export were necessary but no licence was required for parcels, while the legislation of the United States which forbids American export of morphia and opium to China, does not forbid the through traffic of British goods. Here, then, the beginnings of international policy do not appear to have been altogether successful.

As an example of successful international action reference may be made to the Universal Postal Union, which was the most important international organisation before the war, so far as the realities of international life are concerned. It is obvious that (1) communication between persons distant from one another often necessitates transit across many countries and that (2) uncertainty as to rates paid in different countries or by different routes is objectionable.[2] The governments, therefore, eventually agreed to act under an international rule which is fixed by an International Congress deciding by a majority vote.[3] Actually the postal administration of every civilised state obeys the rule of the international authority in regard to foreign post : this international authority is the Congress on which are represented not only the postal administration of sovereign states but also that of some Dependencies. Thus Algeria,

[1] The International Anti-Opium Association is an instance of voluntary effort. *cf.* Dewey, *New Republic*, (December 24, 1919), also *Times*, p. 2, January 3, 1920.

[2] A letter from U.S.A. to Australia before the days of the Postal Union might cost for the half-ounce, 5 cents, 33 cents, 45 cents, 60 cents, and 1 dollar 2 cents according to the route used. Reinsch, " Public International Unions."

[3] Woolf, p. 123.

OFFICIAL INTERNATIONAL ORGANISATION 149

Indo-China and the other French Colonies as one body are given votes and so are the Colonies and Dependencies of Great Britain, which gives the British Empire eight votes. In practice, however, the eight British votes have not always been given on the same side. The permanent Bureau is paid for by contributions of the member states, divided for this purpose into seven classes in accordance with their probable use of foreign correspondence.

The principles upon which the Postal Union works are laid down in the Convention revised in 1906 :[1] and the most important of these principles are :—

1. The countries in the Union form a single postal territory for exchange of correspondence.

2. Freedom of transit is guaranteed throughout the territory of the Union. The transit charges are fixed according to the total net weight and according to the mileage of transit. The basis for charges is obtained by weighing mails during four weeks every six years.

3. Uniform postal rates for foreign correspondence are fixed.

4. In case of loss the responsibility of Administrations is established.

5. Acceptance for transit through the post of certain articles is forbidden.

6. Restricted unions for special purposes are allowed.

7. Arbitration in disputes between Administrations is provided for.

The Postal Union has continued to operate throughout the war and its administrations will eventually be co-ordinated with that of the League of Nations. It will therefore add to the League the long experience of actual international administrative organisation ; and it is well to remember that every postman is in a sense an international official since he is carrying out, for part of his duties, rules laid down by the Universal Postal Union. It is proved, then, that communication can be organised by an international body so as to cover the whole world. In 1910 the number of letters carried under the international rule was 905 millions, of post cards 277 millions, of printed matter 551 millions, and all this means a large increase in international life.

Another instance of international action in regard to communication is the Railway Freight Bureau, which

[1] Woolf, p. 120.

controls for public service the railway freight on "through" lines between nine European states.[1]

Another natural sphere for international action is protection from epidemic disease.[2] It has been found quite impossible to exclude epidemics from any country so long as that country acted alone. The movement of goods and of people in modern times much increases the danger to every nation; and in fact Europe had a recurrence of cholera epidemics in 1830, 1848, 1851, 1865, 1884 and 1892. The early attempt of each nation by quarantine to segregate itself was proved a failure, both because it put obstacles in the way of commerce and because no state acting alone had enough information as to when and where the epidemic disease existed. The states were compelled to take joint action and a Convention was signed in 1903, which provides for the international notification of diseases, the regulation of certain dangerous merchandise, and stated periods of quarantine, as well as rules for receiving ships in harbour. International Sanitary Councils were set up to supervise certain Eastern trade routes; and an international office of Public Health was established in Paris to collect documents and information.

The Danube Commission is an instance of a permanent international body for a restricted administrative area.[3] The Commission held its first meeting on November 4th, 1856, and had to deal with a river passing through many states, obstructed by all kinds of shoals, and yet an important trade route for other nations besides those controlling its banks. Therefore the International Commission set up under the treaty of Paris had representatives of Austria, France, Great Britain, Prussia, Russia, Sardinia and Turkey; it had eventually in 1883 complete administrative control of the whole Danube as far as the Iron Gates. It cleared shoals, placed lights and immensely increased the trade on the river. It is, therefore, an example of successful international administration.[4]

Similar international administration was forced upon the Allies during the recent great war. The purchase of food

[1] Woolf, "International Government," p. 137.
[2] Woolf, p. 140.
[3] cf. L. S. Woolf, "The Future of Constantinople," in which a full account is given of the Danube Commission.
[4] Intermediate between separate sovereignty and international administration is "Condominium," which, as far as results in the New Hebrides are evidence, is proved to be a failure.

OFFICIAL INTERNATIONAL ORGANISATION

stufts and raw material for war uses was affected by bodies representing the States concerned : and at the close of the war, the Allied Maritime Transport Council controlled and allocated all available tonnage. It is true that this experiment was made possible by governmental controls in each nation which were endured for the sake of winning a war : and without war enthusiasm nations do not easily act together. Nevertheless upon such experiments has been built the administrative organisation of the new League of Nations.

The League of Nations

It is outside the purpose of this book either to explain or to advocate an ideal policy in international affairs ; and unfortunately much of what is usually meant by a League of Nations remains in the region of the unrealised ideal.[1] Something, however, has been accomplished ; and this accomplishment must be described, not indeed as a solution of the problems of international politics, but as further machinery for their solution.

It is to be feared that if the machinery turns out to be ineffectual, the cause may be found not in evil intentions of politicians nor in the machinations of " the old diplomacy," but in the ignorance and apathy of the peoples and the absence both from the popular and the official mind of any genuine international policy.

A League of Nations is established under the Peace Treaties. It is therefore necessary, first, to explain the situation thus created by reference to the Treaties and, secondly, to describe the actual experience of the working of the League in its informal and preliminary stage.

The " Covenant " is the name given to Part I of the Peace Treaty with Germany.[2] Apparently the name has religious connections and is intended to give a lofty tone to a badly-drafted legal document ; but it may be hoped that the loftiness of the general conception will not be regarded as a sufficient excuse for the ineffectiveness which has usually characterised moral principles in international affairs.

[1] A brief account of the history of the ideal of a League will be found in my " Political Ideals," 3rd ed., chap. xiii.
[2] The Presbyterian traditions of Mr. Wilson, Mr. Lansing and Colonel House were noted at Paris : and the theological element is emphasised in Keynes' " Economic Consequences of the Peace."

It is to be noted, further, that the agreement founding the League is part of Treaties which contain evidences of vindictiveness, primitive jealousy and political incompetence. Whatever amendments of the Treaties are made in future, the original connections of the League have been detrimental to its prestige : and it may for a long time be doubtful whether the Treaties will damn the League or the League redeem the Treaties or, possibly, whether a separation can be made between the League as the basis of peace and the other provisions of the Treaties as the product of war

The League as established does not embody the attitude of those voluntary associations which prepared schemes during the war. The leading idea is not arbitration and the adjudication of disputes but international administration ; and the Covenant was in fact based upon two drafts prepared at Paris by the British and American delegations. The Peace Conference appointed a Commission on January 25, which met for the first time on February 3 ;[1] and the first draft of the Covenant was presented to the Conference on February 14. The Covenant was redrafted between March 27 and April 10, with a view to finding a possible place for Russia and Germany on the Council and with a view to allowing for the Munroe Doctrine.[2] The signed document founds a League of twenty-seven original members while thirteen other states have been invited to accede. A two-thirds vote of the Assembly will allow admission of other states.

The position will be explained best by describing first the structure of the League ; secondly, the work assigned to the League ; and, thirdly, the methods already adopted for doing the work. The League is obviously an administrative rather than a legislative body ; the Council and not the Assembly is the real power, and in close connection

---

[1] The original Commission contained two representatives of the five Great Powers and one of each for Belgium, Brazil, China, Portugal, and Serbia, to whom were added, on February 6th, Greece, Czecho-Slovakia, Poland and Rumania. The membership indicates the peculiar situation : here was a Commission, not for making terms of settlement with enemies, but for drafting a world-scheme, and yet the only peoples represented were those allied and associated for carrying on a war.

[2] *cf. International Review*, June, 1919, p. 470, note on amendments. *cf.* also Lord E. Percy in " The Peace Conference."

OFFICIAL INTERNATIONAL ORGANISATION 153

with the Council is the Secretariat. Here then a departure is made from the old tradition of the Hague Conference and of International lawyers and the majority of the theorists of internationalism ; but the departure is due to recent political experience. The older political theory over-emphasised legislation ; but experience has shown (1) that it is useless to make laws unless there is an administration to direct their observance, (2) that the application of law by administration is itself a kind of legislation, and that (3) it is better political practice to secure an agreement which is definite enough to be enforceable than the vague consent to a principle of which no one knows the exact meaning. These are principles of politics which are as much applicable to domestic as to international politics and without prejudice it may be said that their discovery is due to British and German administrative development, whereas both in the United States and in some European countries the general acceptance of a vague principle or the mere passing of laws is still overestimated. Whatever the underlying ideas, however, it is clear that the League is in the main administrative.

The Council is a small body representing the governments of " the British Empire," France, Italy, Japan, and until the Assembly decides otherwise, Belgium, Brazil, Greece and Spain. It is to meet " from time to time " and at least once a year.

The first meeting of the Council was held on January 11, 1920, and this was regarded as the formal inception of the League. The representatives of the Governments on the Council will naturally obey the orders and maintain the policies of their several Governments and therefore the Council is not in any sense superior to the constituent states : it is in fact a development of the older Conferences of ambassadors, and at most it cannot do more than a council of governors or representatives in a very loose confederation. Again, the policy of the Council, if it has any policy of its own, will inevitably be dictated by the policy or policies of the most powerful Great Powers represented on the Council : if it is not so dictated, the Council must have either no policy at all or a merely abstract and ineffective policy.

It is impossible to say whether this situation is good or bad. The merely abstract ideal of world-government is futile : no large group of men under a government of their own choosing or one in which they acquiesce is likely to consent to be instruments of a policy dictated by representatives of many or few other groups. On the other hand there is a danger that the Council may become the executive of a few powerful states dictating to other and smaller states, which even if incapable of right action may nevertheless feel that they would prefer to do as they will. The political value of the Council, therefore, cannot be estimated on abstract grounds but only when the policy of the Council has actually been experienced; for it is possible that even Great Powers may be capable of substituting for foreign politics a genuine international politics.

The Assembly is to meet " at stated intervals " but the intervals have not so far been stated; and it is to consist of representatives of the states, but although each state may send three, the voting is to be one for each state.[1] The Assembly votes on the admission of new members to the League, and as already in November 1919 Germany and Austria were admitted by the International Labour Conference at Washington, they will probably be admitted to the League. The Assembly also selects four of the minor representatives on the Council and it may (Article XIV) refer questions to the International Court. It is, however, neither a parliament nor a committee and in the present form of the agreement cannot very well be more than a general meeting for public speeches. It is hardly even a concession to the desire of some for a world parliament, for some of the governments it represents are more effectually represented on the Council and the others are represented as empty voices. The Council remains absolutely dominant.

Attached to the Council is the Director General of the League,[2] who selects and controls a Secretariat: and this Secretariat carries on the continuous administrative work of the League, the Council and the Secretariat forming a body like the Allied Maritime Transport Council and its permanent secretaries. This is a situation entirely different from that of the pre-war international bureaux, both because the Council is not merely consultative and because the Secretariat has definite administrative func-

[1] Decisions of Council or Assembly must be unanimous (Art. V) except in the case of admitting new members of the League.
[2] Sir James Eric Drummond, named in the Annex.

OFFICIAL INTERNATIONAL ORGANISATION

tions and a higher status than the officials of the old bureaux.

The organisation of the Secretariat indicates the range of the League's possible activities. Under the Secretary General (British) there are under-Secretaries (French, Italian and Japanese) and under them fourteen directors, others to be added dealing with armaments, the drug traffic, etc. At its inception the office contained (1) a political section with geographical divisions, reviewing all political questions likely to lead to disputes; (2) an economic section dealing with Article 23 E, the equitable treatment of the commerce of all nations and with the economic boycott and connecting with the League any international economic organisations which may exist; (3) a legal section, dealing with the revision of treaties under Article 19, and the setting up of a Permanent Court; (4) a bureaux section co-ordinating all official international bureaux and connecting with voluntary international associations; (5) a mandatory section, for mandates under Article 22; (6) an Administrative Commissions section, for co-ordinating the work of the Commissions for the Saar Valley, Danzig, etc.

The work assigned to the League is of two kinds (1) international and constructive or (2) maintenance of certain sections of the Treaties of Peace. Under the first head comes (a) the reduction of armaments (Article VIII); but here the Council is only to propose what no government is bound to carry out. Nevertheless it is agreed in the text signed by the governments that there are " grave objections to the manufacture by private enterprise of munitions and implements of war." Such sentiments invoke Aristophanes. Again (b) in case of a danger of war the Council is to be called (Article XI) following the plan of the London Conference and the unsuccessful suggestions of the British Foreign Minister before the outbreak of the great war. Further (c) arbitration, inquiry by the Council (Article XII) and a Court (Article XIV) are established: a distinction is made between disputes suitable for arbitration (justiciable) and those not suitable, which are dealt with by the publication of a report from the Council (Article XV). There is to be (d) joint action by members of the League against any member resorting to war without using the machinery provided, as Italy did against Turkey in 1911 in spite of the Hague Convention. There is here, however, and in other articles (Article XX) an acknowledgment of a certain common interest among all the members of the League and machinery is devised for keeping treaties registered and revised as well as co-ordinating all international bureaux under the League. Finally (e) it may be counted an international act to supervise " mandates."

Article 22 of the Covenant deals with the Mandatory system. It is applicable only to the ex-German colonies and for a time to certain liberated communities hitherto under Turkish rule. With regard to the former it is said that " the principle should be applied" that the future of such peoples " forms a sacred trust of civilisation." They are to be in tutelage of advanced nations, who are to be called Mandatories, on behalf of the League. In the abstract it is agreed that the question as to which state is to be mandatory for any people should be answered by reference to its " experience or geographical position"; and when the mandated territory is sparsely populated and near the territory of the Mandatory, the latter may administer it " as an integral portion " of its own territory. Thus South-West Africa and the South Pacific Islands become, in effect, parts of the British Dominions, South Africa and Australia.

The other ex-German colonies are Togoland, Cameroons and East Africa. It might be imagined that the kind of authority of the governing state would be decided by the League of Nations in regard at least to these: but the Covenant indicates that this is necessary only " if not previously agreed upon by the Members of the League," and, as a matter of fact, these territories are already administered by France, Belgium, Portugal and Great Britain. Therefore although the Mandatory System may indicate good-will, there is little to distinguish it from the old-fashioned " possession " of territory.

It is to be noted that in regard to the African and Pacific territories there is no mention made in the Covenant of " the wishes of the inhabitants ": the government of these peoples is to be decided by others. In regard, however, to ex-Turkish territories, Armenia, Syria, etc., the Covenant says that " the wishes of these communities must be a *principal* consideration in the selection of a Mandatory." Here, therefore, the peoples are to have some power to choose their governors, but that power is very small; for many other considerations, besides the "principal" consideration, exist: and further, the reservation apparently applies to this case also that arrangements made "previously" will hold, to the exclusion of any definition of the Mandatories' authorities by the Council of the League.

The Mandatory is bound to render to the Council an annual report on the mandated area; but there are no other defined duties, except the vague acceptance of the government as a sacred trust—whatever that may be. The execution of heretics by the Spanish Inquisition was believed to be the carrying out of a sacred trust: and the Holy Alliance restored incompetent autocrats as a sacred trust. It has, indeed, been remarked that if in the eighteenth century, Frederick II, Maria Theresa and Catherine II had been in advance of their times, they would have given, one to the other, the mandates for different parts of Poland.[1]

It is clear, however, that the idea of responsibility for the administration of native territories is of supreme international importance. The forms of a "mandate" cannot be in doubt: the dangers of government in undeveloped countries are sufficiently well known and even if the mandatory system involves nothing more than an extension of the old system of protectorates, it will inevitably tend to level up the practice of all governments because they have accepted the idea that a certain moral and political standard exists in this regard.[2]

As for the non-international maintenance of the terms of treaties, the League and its Council act as agents of the late Allied and Associated Powers. The most striking instance is (Art. X) the maintenance of the "territorial

[1] The idea of mandates and even the use of the word is, of course, to be found outside the Treaties, as, for example, in the Message of President Roosevelt, January 4, 1904. "If ever a government could be said to have received a mandate from civilisation to effect an object the accomplishment of which was demanded by the interest of mankind, the United States holds that position with regard to the inter-oceanic canal. . . . That our position as the mandatory of civilisation has been by no means misconceived is shown by the promptitude with which the Powers have, one after another, followed our lead in recognising Panama as an independent state."

[2] The scheme for a mandate drawn up by the Anti-Slavery Society is published as a leaflet, and in the *International Review*, October, 1919, *cf.* below, p. 165.

integrity" of all its members of the League :[1] but the Covenant itself does not contain any other instance of partisan duties to be performed by the League. It was, nevertheless, found convenient to place upon the League such tasks as that of administering the Saar coalfield (Art. 49 and subsection 17 of Annex), judgment on the separateness of Austria (Art. 80), the control of Danzig (Art. 102), control of German armaments (Art. 164); and the German Treaty, indeed, gives the impression that the League was remembered occasionally although happily forgotten in the case of some of the plebiscites and of "reparation."

Criticism of the League, its Council and its functions is not necessary here; it is a fact of international politics which is new enough to be left for the present at least uncondemned. The whole system, however, has obviously been affected by the influence of enemies of international co-operation and whatever constructive policy is embodied in the scheme is due to the effort of a few who were not greatly helped by popular opinion. The end of a war is obviously no time to establish peace; for the warmind is dominant: and yet if this much were not done while some among the peoples still remembered, many years might have passed without any revival of interest in any political issues which were not domestic.

The International Labour Organisation.

The Labour Parties of some of the countries allied against the Central Empires had frequently during the war advocated the holding of an international Labour Conference at the same time as the Peace Conference. For various reasons, but chiefly because the Labour Parties at the end of the war were in opposition to the Governments, it was decided by the Governments that no separate Labour Conference could be held. It was, however, found possible to appoint a special Labour Commission in Paris for the drafting of clauses to be inserted into the Peace Treaty with Germany.

The result of the Commission's work was what is now Part XIII of the Treaty with Germany; and this part

[1] It is notorious that the United States Senate made a difficulty as to maintaining the territories acquired by the Allies or the new states.

OFFICIAL INTERNATIONAL ORGANISATION

suffers, as the first part does, both from its connection with the territorial and economic clauses of the Treaty and from the unprecedented refusal on the part of the Allied Governments to allow to Germany any discussion or joint conferences on the subjects dealt with. The Labour section of the Treaty has, however, set up an international organisation which is operative.

It was at one time expected that the Treaty would contain provisions as to labour conditions; but in fact these conditions are referred to only in the preamble to Part XIII and there only as the reasons for setting up legislative and administrative organisation of an international character. The most important fact, therefore, for international politics is this new organisation. In connection with the League of Nations as already described an International Labour Organisation is established including (1) a quasi-legislative Conference, (2) a permanent committee called a Governing Body, and (3) an administrative office.

The international Conference has already met once at Washington (Oct. 29, Nov. 29, 1919) and has passed certain Conventions, Recommendations and Resolutions in regard to (1) the eight-hour day and forty-eight hour week, (2) unemployment, (3) the regulation of women's labour before and after child-birth, during the night and in dangerous occupations, (4) the regulation of juvenile labour in regard to the school age.[1]

The Conference consists of representatives from the various administrations which are parties to the Convention embodied in the Peace Treaty. Some of these administrations are governments of sovereign states: but Australia, Canada, South Africa, New Zealand and India are given equal status with the sovereign states. The representatives from each administration are four, two representing the Government, one the employers and one organised labour : but the delegates do not form one group for each administration and indeed at the first conference the voting was not by national divisions but by divisions cutting across the national or state group.

The General Conference has the following powers.

[1] Three reports on these questions were issued by the International Organising Committee for the Washington Conference. The reports contain reviews of the legislative and administrative position in regard to these questions in about forty-five different countries.

It controls the whole Labour Organisation (the Governing Body and Secretariat), independently of the Assembly or the Council of the League of Nations. It can pass Conventions or other agreements by majority votes. It has the right to have its conventions and agreements presented by the several Governments to their several legislatures, although it has no power to bind these Governments or legislatures to take any action to enforce the conventions or agreements.

The Governing Body is a committee for the control of the international Labour Office which will be set up at the seat of the League of Nations. According to the Treaty it is to consist of representatives from the eight states of chief industrial importance and from four other states to be chosen by the General Conference. Besides representatives of Governments, the Governing Body contains six representatives of employers and six of organised workers, and is therefore partially a " functional " as opposed to a territorial body.

The Secretariat of the international Labour Office is under the Director General, who is controlled by the Governing Body and the General Conference and is not subordinated to the Secretary General of the League of Nations. The Director and his staff are paid through the Secretary General, but under provisions made by the General Conference which the Secretary General has no power to limit or control.

Some interesting conclusions can be drawn from the structure of this international organisation. In the first place, the principle of the representation of *interests* as opposed to localities, has been admitted and is operative: the General Conference is not an organ of the state-system only but does include other systems such as the economic union of employers and the trade union system on an international scale. It is, therefore, different from Parliaments and if successful it may even affect the Parliamentary system in the several states where industrial organisation is not of a status equal to the political. Secondly, in regard to labour matters the League has a separate and special quasi-legislature and administration: but there is no reason why the same principle should not operate in regard to other than labour matters.

Official international organisation has developed rapidly during the past century, and it is obvious now that the

OFFICIAL INTERNATIONAL ORGANISATION 161

international relations of modern states no longer involve only or chiefly the arbitration of disputes. Governments have now learnt to act together for joint interests and administration of a new kind has been proved successful. The state, then, clearly is no longer an atomic and segregate political unit : it can, for certain purposes, become a part of a larger unit without destroying any of its character or utility to its own citizens. Indeed the substitution of international joint action for a mere conflict of foreign policies has been proved to be beneficial to the citizens of the states concerned. The development of international organisation has been varied and complex in the sphere of communications, health, police and the rest.

The League of Nations is sometimes spoken of as the culmination of the process. This, however, is misleading. As at present organised the League is too simple and too inclusive : for the phenomena of international politics seem to demand a larger development of the principle embodied in the Labour clauses of the Treaties. Indeed it would perhaps have been better if many various international organisations for distinct purposes had been established and only a very loose co-ordination or federation of all of them attempted. There might then have been a place for the special representation and administration of the several distinct international interests in finance, commerce, transport, undeveloped countries and the rest. The League might, then, have been a co-ordination of all these. It would more easily have avoided the dangers of the Great State system and administrative functional centralisation : and it would have been less closely connected with the Supreme Council of the Allies which has dominated Europe since the close of the war.

CHAPTER VIII

UNOFFICIAL INTERNATIONAL ORGANISATIONS

IT would not be possible to understand the life of any people or race by studying merely the organisation of their government: and indeed it would hardly be possible to understand the nature of that government without reference to the larger sphere of unofficial organisation, prevailing customs or habits of mind and the various sections of life which are not as yet organised or may not be susceptible of organisation. Politics covers only a small part of social life. International politics, in the same way, covers only a part of international life: and even that section cannot be understood without reference to a wider field of voluntary effort and unorganised vitality.

Unofficial organisation of international life has developed very rapidly since the beginning of the nineteenth century. By comparison with diplomacy and diplomatic organs, it is recent; but it is already almost as powerful. Unfortunately organisation has too often been connected in the minds of progressive thinkers with the state only; and not enough use has been made of the principle of voluntary association and specific, non-governmental administration in the international sphere. Reformers have tended to look too much to governments, from which indeed in the international sphere if not otherwise most of the evils come. It is true that unless the states and their governments cease to be armed bands acting with deliberate fraud in the name of national interests, there will not be any development of international civilisation. It is true that governments and the states of which they are the executive agents aim theoretically at justice and liberty, which cannot be secured unless all states act together for that purpose. But the reform of state-life may best come through the development of a life independent of the state: for the state is only one among many institutions and by no means the best; and even for the development of official organisation

UNOFFICIAL INTERNATIONAL ORGANISATIONS

voluntary associations are probably the most effective instruments.

Further, the promotion of international life cannot be delayed until the armament trade dies down and foreign policy becomes international policy. Many useful functions in the international sphere can even now be performed without the initiative or even the assistance of governments: and therefore it is necessary to review the non-official organisations of various types, in order to see what is being done and what remains to be done.

There are some sections of human knowledge and action which not even the most foolish can believe to be national. Mathematics and physical science cannot seriously be supposed to differ in different countries or among different peoples: and it cannot be disputed that the general store of such knowledge is increased by the interchange of ideas among men of different races, languages and religions. Some parts of physical science, indeed, cannot progress at all except by joint investigation of men in many lands: astronomy, for example, necessitates international co-operation and there are many international associations already formed.[1] Unfortunately for national or imperial self-sufficiency, it appears to be impossible for any nation to prevent other nations seeing the same sun and stars. Again, the mapping of the Earth and the oceans and the recording of earthquakes, necessitate international co-operation, for which also there are special associations.[2]

Further, in the practical application of science to health it has been found necessary for nations to co-operate and there are international associations or congresses for tuberculosis, surgery, anatomy, embryology and many other sections of medical science, partly co-ordinated by a Permanent International Commission of International Congresses of Medicine. Examples of the use by each nation of the discoveries or skill of foreigners are to be found in the universal use of anti-septic and a-septic treatment, most of the modern drugs, and methods of psychiatry and diet.

Art, which is sometimes too simply conceived as national in character, also owes much to international contacts. In drama, Ibsen and the older writers, in music, Beethoven,

[1] Central Bureau of Astronomical Telegrams, 1882.
[2] International Union for Co-operation in Solar Research, 1904. International Committee for the Map of the Sky.

Brahms, Dvorak and others, in painting and sculpture, Cezanne and Rodin, all have international influence : and no nation at present has a great art which is not due in part to the skill and insight of foreigners.

In trade and commerce it has been already shown in a former chapter that different industries and services tend to organisation on an international scale ; and this implies not merely a dangerous power of a new grouping but the greater availability of the brains and resources of many nations in a common service of production and distribution. All the instances, however, referred to above are unions for the sake of the financial gain of those who control them. It is interesting therefore to note that there is also a non-financial internationalism affecting trade and commerce. There are periodic international Congresses of Chambers of Commerce ; international Congresses of Electricians for the arrangement of common standards of measurement and material, an international Electro-technical Commission (1906), an international Petrol Commission, an international Association for testing Materials (metals, stones, etc.).

Most of these international associations are supported by governments ; but they are due to voluntary unofficial efforts of persons interested in the different subjects, who find in practice that they cannot make progress without international co-operation. They represent, therefore, the conscious need for joint action between men of different races, languages and traditions.

There are many international associations which, although voluntary and unofficial, have close connections with Governments. For example, the International Association for Labour Legislation founded in 1900, consists of thirteen national sections of which the members are persons interested in social reforms. The purpose of the Association was to press the Government to action and through this voluntary effort the Convention of 1906 was signed forbidding night-work for women, and another Convention was in process of being agreed in 1913. The Association, however, may be counted as almost official, since most of the money on which it depended was contributed by the Governments.

Another example is the International Maritime Committee formed in 1898, on which seventeen nations were represented.[1] The members were not officials but repre-

[1] Woolf, " International Government," p. 169 *seq.*

sentatives of shipowners in the different nations: the Committee however aimed at promoting governmental action in regard to maritime law. Through their activity diplomatic conferences met in 1905, 1909 and 1910, and two conventions framed by the Committee were signed by almost all the maritime states. These Conventions unified the laws on Salvage and Collisions at Sea.

Another form of international association is to be found in the inter-parliamentary Union, which was founded in 1889 and was originally intended to co-ordinate the policy in the several representative Chambers of promoting international arbitration of disputes. It prepared a draft in 1895 which was the basis for the establishment in 1899 of the Hague Court of arbitration. It held eighteen conferences before the war and supported its own international Bureau. In 1914 it included twenty-four national groups with about 3,500 individual representatives and various Governments supply it with funds.

In these cases the unofficial associations promote official action and, of course, it is a common phenomenon of politics that governments should be so galvanised into action. Agitation and the pressure of organised opinion are active in the international as in the domestic sphere. There is, however, a very large place for non-official organisation which exists for purposes which governments do not pursue.

In direct reference to the action of governments, but by no means invariably with governmental approval, are such international associations as those for the protection of native races. Reform has already been secured by such societies; and if there is to be any force in the machine of the "Mandatory" system, it must come from such unofficial sources. There is at Geneva an international Bureau for the protection of native races which co-ordinates the information and activities of various national bodies. A Swiss League concerns itself chiefly with the Belgian Congo, a French League chiefly with the French Congo, a Peruvian League at Lima chiefly with Putumayo, and the British Anti-Slavery Society chiefly with Rhodesia and other British dependencies: but all these bodies have similar general policies opposed to the concessionaire system, forced labour and the displacement of natives from the land.[1]

[1] cf. F. Challaye, "Le Congo Français": general information from the Bureau International des Ligues de Defense des Indigènes, 29, Chemin de Miremount, Champel, Geneva.

The Red Cross Societies are another instance of a real internationalism. There are at present two international organisations of these societies. The older, the international Committee, is the intermediary between the various national Red Cross societies, and if war breaks out the societies of belligerent states still communicate through this committee: but the committee like the Red Cross Societies has hitherto worked only for armies in the field or for prisoners of war. Civilian needs, especially in disasters or epidemics have, however, been dealt with by the Red Cross Societies of U.S.A., Italy and Japan: and it is now certain that the whole of the Red Cross organisation will be concerned with this peace work. The new international League of Red Cross Societies, formed in 1919 by societies of France, Great Britain, Italy, Japan and U.S.A., is devoted to a peace-time programme complementary to that of the international Committee. It aims at international voluntary organisation for preventing disease and mitigating suffering, making known new medico-scientific knowledge and co-ordinating relief work.[1] Both the international Committee and the League have their central offices at Geneva. The work already done has proved the value of the organisations. The Red Cross on the battle-field and the work for prisoners of war is well known, but since the war great work has been done by the League, for example, in Poland both directly and by inciting the Government to act. The League sent a Commission to Poland in August 1919, and the report on the typhus epidemic was the cause of further measures of relief. Lack of food, clothing and soap was increasing everywhere the most deadly forms of disease and, as the Commission said, "even in the present situation which restricts travel and commerce there is a considerable movement of people to and from Poland to Western Europe ... and many thousands are waiting an opportunity to migrate. In Poland there are several thousand American citizens in the army waiting to return as well as many French ex-prisoners of war awaiting repatriation." Holland and Genoa have already had slight epidemics of typhus.[2]

[1] These are almost the phrases of the Articles of Association of the League. I owe this information to the kindness of Lt.-Col. F. A. Earle, of the British Red Cross Society: 28 countries are now (January, 1919) represented in the League, which publishes a Bulletin at Geneva.
[2] Report in Bulletin I, No. 4, October 1919.

UNOFFICIAL INTERNATIONAL ORGANISATIONS

The situation, therefore, apart from sympathy, calls for international action to protect uninfected areas and our own countries.[1]

Genuine international action has been taken by the Friends' Emergency and War Victims' Relief Committee. After good work done during the war, visits were paid to Poland, Germany and Austria.[2] On February 2, the Supreme Economic Council gave permission to send food and clothing into Germany. In May 1919 a medical unit was sent to Zawiercie in Poland. On June 28, the first goods were dispatched for V___na and in November there were twenty workers from the Committee in that city. The efforts made were not confined to almsgiving: for the organisation of the milk supply and of transport, the restoration of credit and the re-organisation of industry were all promoted by the Friends. The American Friends did similar work and both in Switzerland and in Holland arrangements were made to receive and to feed for short periods the starving children of Germany and Austria.

The Labour Internationals

Outside the province of state action there has been a considerable growth of international organisation of the "workers." Probably it is felt that the workers of any one nation may be injured by what is done to the workers of another nation: for example the cotton spinners of Lancashire may be injured by the under-payment of cotton spinners in Japan.[3] There is also the common hope among all workers that the present industrial and social system may be transformed into a better system; and it is felt that since the present system is organised internationally, the attack upon it should also be organised internationally. A common distress and a common hope have thus united the workers of many countries, although the union is still weak, easily broken and never very vigorously maintained by the rank and file in any nation.

[1] Bulletin, October 1919, p. 10.

[2] From January 23rd until September 30th, 1919, the amount raised by the Committee was £82,714.

[3] cf. Cmd. 511 (1920), Japanese Labour. In 1916 there were 4,395 girls under 12 years old in the textile factories, and 460,735 women over 15. Trade unions are non-existent; a Law forbids instigating a strike (p.19). Cotton spinners are recruited by agents in country districts. The recruits are girls of 16 to 22, who are housed on the mill premises: the machines run night and day and the girls work in two shifts of 10 to 12 hours (p. 16).

The two branches of labour organisation are, as in national affairs, political and industrial: and internationally as in national life, the industrial organisation is based upon trade unions or craft associations.

Politically the international socialist movement is the most important fact. The first Congress was held in London in 1847, but the Communist League then founded did not survive after 1852. Ten years afterwards meetings were held in London from which resulted the International Association of Working Men: and a congress was held at Geneva in 1866, but the organisation did not survive after 1873. Again in 1889, new International Socialist Congresses were held at Paris; but there was some disagreement between the different forms of Socialism. The International Socialist Bureau was, however, established at a congress at Paris in 1900, and the chief office was established at Brussels. Twenty-eight national groups were represented in the Bureau before the war. Congresses were held at Amsterdam (1904), Stuttgart (1907) and Copenhagen (1910). A special congress was held at Basle in November 1912 which was attended by 555 delegates, to protest against the participation of the Great Powers in the Balkan War.[1] The next Congress was to have been held in Vienna in 1914; but the war made this impossible.

The most important indication of the tendency of the movement in international politics is to be found in the resolution passed at the Congress of 1907 which runs as follows: " If war threatens to break out it is the duty of the working class in the countries concerned and of their Parliamentary representatives, with the help of the International Socialist Bureau as a means of co-ordinating their action, to use every effort to prevent war by all the means which seem to them most appropriate, having regard to the sharpness of the class war and to the general political situation. Should war, none the less, break out, their duty is to intervene to bring it promptly to an end, and with all their energies to use the political and economic crisis created by the war to rouse the populace from its slumbers and to hasten the fall of capitalist domination." [2]

[1] *Labour Year Book*, 1916, p. 407.
[2] G. D. H. Cole, " Labour in War-time,": chapter on " War and Class War."

UNOFFICIAL INTERNATIONAL ORGANISATIONS 169

At the beginning of the war the International Socialist movement was committed to the policy of their 1907 resolution ; but the efforts of socialist groups was in fact absorbed in the general excitement of the belligerent nations, and nothing was done internationally until through the Dutch and Scandinavian sections an invitation was issued to an international labour Conference at Stockholm in 1917. This Conference was made impossible by the general political atmosphere and the action of some governments. Meantime conferences of the more extreme socialists had been held at Zimmerwald (Sept. 1915) and Kienthal (April, 1916) ; while inter-allied conferences in London (Feb. 1915, Feb. 20th, 1918, Sept. 17th, 1918) kept the idea of international action alive.[1]

At the close of the war a revival of the old International took place at a meeting at Berne (Jan. 26-Feb. 10th, 1919) :[2] but by this time disagreement had shown itself among socialists, and a " Third " International had been founded by the Soviet authorities in Moscow. To this Third International the Italian Socialist Party, the Independents of Germany and some smaller groups in other countries, gave their adhesion ; and the difficulties arising from this division of forces have not yet been solved.

The industrial side of the labour movement is represented in international politics by the International Federation of Trade Unions, founded in 1901. About twenty countries are represented ;[3] but little has been attempted except the improvement of the knowledge of the trade union movement in the whole world. Conferences were held in 1903 and 1909, and in 1912 there were nineteen countries affiliated through organisations including about 7,000,000 members.

[1] *Labour Year Book*, 1919, " Internationalism and the International," p. 41.

[2] A permanent Commission of the International, meeting at Amsterdam (April 26, 1919) issued resolutions in regard to territorial changes (Georgia, Esthonia, etc.). The Constitution of the new " Second " International will be found in Appendix X of the Report of the Executive of the British Labour Party for June 25, 1919.

[3] Before the war Great Britain was represented by the General Federation of Trade Unions, which included in January 1919 only 1,214,000 members of union. The Trade Union Congress was not represented on the International Federation, but is now. It may be gathered that the International Federation was not powerful, as its total expenditure was less than £600 a year.

After the war a preliminary Conference was held at Berne in Feb. 1919; and a more important Conference at Amsterdam on 26th July, 1919, when a new constitution was agreed, by which the voting is not to be by national units but on the basis of a proportion between the number of members of the organisations represented and the number of votes. The purpose is to give due weight to countries of greater industrial importance: but the Trade Union International like the Socialist International has been confused in its policies by the episodes of the war and, in any case, no industrial or economic action on an international scale appears to result from the Federation's meetings. The movement may be significant of a tendency; but it is industrially ineffectual at present.

International federations exist in special industries;[1] but most of them are only for the purpose of holding periodical conferences at which information can be communicated from one national group to the other. The International Miners' Federation originally united miners' unions of seven countries, including 1,374,000 members; the Metal Workers' Federation united eighteen countries and had 1,106,000 members. Since the armistice of 1918 there has been a renewal of these International Federations; and an even more significant movement is the alliance of unions in different countries with a view to joint industrial action of an international character or at least to mutual support in finance and policy.[2]

The movement of workers across frontiers has tended to spread the power of trade union organisation. For example, some British Trade Unions have branches abroad. The A.S.E. have 210 branches outside the United Kingdom, and the Amalgamated Society of Carpenters and Joiners, 161. Most of these are in the Dominions; but there are 42 A.S.E. and 50 Carpenters and Joiners branches in the United States. The A.S.E. has one non-English speaking branch in Spain. The Steam Engine Makers' Society and the United Society of Boilermakers also have branches outside the United Kingdom.

[1] Before the war there were 32: *cf. Labour Year Book*, 1916 p. 431. Woolf, "International Government," p. 211 *seq*.
[2] For example, the Workers' Union of Great Britain has entered into close relations with unions in Belgium and France. In August 1919 a conference was held in Paris representing Postal workers of Belgium, France, Great Britain and Spain.

No foreign unions appear to have branches in the United Kingdom except that of the Swiss Hotel Employees.

In the U.S.A. and Canada the workers in both countries are frequently in the same "international" unions, in spite of the efforts of the Canadian employers to keep the workers in purely "national" or Canadian unions.[1] The Dominion Trade and Labour Congress (1884) is a branch of the American Federation of Labour, and since 1902 it has refused membership to purely local unions not affiliated to the international associations.[2] In 1903, of 1,500 local unions in Canada, 1,300 were so affiliated. The present organisation aims at preventing the introduction of strike breakers from one country into the other. Some unions of the U.S.A. have organised local unions affiliated to those of Mexico, Porto Rico, Hawaii, Alaska and the Canal Zone. There is a branch of the U.S.A. Electrical Workers in the Philippines: but so far there is no world organisation of industrial workers for industrial ends.

International agreements have been entered into by various craft unions. For example, in 1872 an agreement was made between the Iron Moulders' Union of North America and the Friendly Society of Ironfounders of Great Britain by which journeymen bearing cards from the British union would be admitted without entrance fee into the American union. The understanding, however, goes further, for in 1882, when the boiler makers and ship builders of New York went on strike and the employers sent to England for men, the American union cabled to the British and not a man left England.[3] The remission of entrance fees is agreed between the painters' organisations of Germany, Austria, Denmark, Serbia and Switzerland: and a similar agreement holds between unions in the lace industry in England, France and Spain. But unions in the U.S.A. have been slow to make agreements of this kind: and in consequence British unions

[1] T. W. Glocker, "American Trade Unions," 1913, p. 77. The author says that the clergy also opposed international organisations. It will be noted that "international" in reference to U.S.A. and Canada only includes those two countries and outlying districts in America.

[2] Except in the case of unions of Government employees in Canada.

[3] Glocker, *op. cit.*, p. 85.

such as the Carpenters and Joiners set up their own branches in the U.S.A., creating thereby some friction with the local unions.

The tendencies point to (1) a more widely extended use of the trade card for entrance of an immigrant trade unionist into the union of his new country ; (2) a closer confederation of the various national associations in the same trades ; (3) a general organisation for the whole world, including representatives of all trades union groups in all countries.

The organisation of labour on an international scale is still very inadequate ; but the strength of the international feeling is undoubted. The situation is somewhat like that of the early Christians when they had their local organisations and a world-embracing sentiment but when the great mediaeval Church had not yet developed. Whatever the weakness of international labour organisation, therefore, the movement must be reckoned as one of the most important factors in international politics. The purposes implied in the universal sentiment of organised labour in all countries are different in detail but fundamentally uniform. There is an almost universal opposition to the institution called war : there is a universal suspicion of the foreign policies of governments and a universal if more vaguely felt hatred of the sacrifice of human happiness in any country to the development of its natural resources. These however are large political issues which will not be frankly faced until the political power of labour organisations begins to be felt in the foreign policies of governments.

Apart altogether from general policy there are many purposes for which united action by industrial workers of all countries is necessary. For example, there are measures of social amelioration in every country which can best be secured if many states act together in the matter, as it has already been pointed out with regard to the night work of women and the use of white phosphorus in matches : but state action is speedier if there is pressure from organised labour. The machinery, however, for effecting similar reforms in different states is still rather national than international.

The national machinery cannot be so useful in the case of emigrants. In this case there are improvements necessary in regard to accident insurance and unemployment insurance.[1] Foreign workers are not always able to benefit on the same terms as nationals under the insurance schemes and in some countries the insurance schemes are inadequate or restricted. The whole of this section of reform, however, may be regarded as having passed under the supervision of the official International Labour Organisation which is described above.

There are some less definite purposes which can only be attained by voluntary associations : for example, the practice of banishment or outlawry appears to be revived against trade union leaders. Early in 1914 the South African Government removed strike leaders to England ; and the practice of deportation has increased during the war. Obviously pressure of an international character is the best if not the only means of securing that deportation should not occur unless under due legal process for specified reasons and with the full consent of the country to which the deportee is sent. Again the trade union rights of foreign workers are sometimes restricted, as for example by the French law of 1884 which makes it necessary that all officials in French trade unions shall be French nationals, and in the case of the colonies prohibits the membership of aliens or immigrants in local trade unions. These are instances of problems which can hardly be dealt with except by international action ; and it is easily understood that although the method of progress may in some cases be through the influence exerted by labour organisation on governmental action, there remains a large field in which independent action for reform can be effective for solving international problems. Thus outside the diplomatic and governmental sphere of international politics, international life develops unofficial organisations and associations.

The position of all these associations has not been made less important by the establishment of a co-ordinating official department under the League of Nations : on the contrary, it is all the more important now that international life should not be left entirely in official hands ; for the more highly centralised the organs of government, the more important it is that different social functions should be performed by diverse and independent bodies. Again, the official organisation is, as it were,

[1] In 1916 there were fourteen agreements between pairs of states as to the mutual insurance of workers against accidents.

the machine: but voluntary associations provide the driving force. The free and unofficial associations for trade or labour, the various scientific unions and active independent groups such as the Red Cross, have an immense sphere of usefulness both in galvanising officials into committing themselves to a policy and in proceeding with work unsuitable for governmental offices.

The whole situation, however, depends upon the strength and intelligence of public opinion in regard to international affairs. The organisation and development of that opinion is, therefore, a fundamental problem. Undoubtedly political opinion should grow of itself out of the contact between men and the influence upon men of the circumstances in which they find themselves: and if the description given in this book of the various contacts of peoples is correct, there is sufficient ground for the growth in every civilised country of an enlightened public opinion on international affairs. The field, however, is not entirely open. Opinion is already organised, manipulated, developed or distorted by the Press.

The Press is in one sense a means for organising the relations of different peoples: in another sense it is a great problem of international politics. Undoubtedly any Press is an advantage which our forefathers did not possess: and it is better to have even a Press full of lies and irrational prejudices than none at all, since it may possibly induce people to think of events occurring not under their noses; and a cynic might argue also that an obviously bad Press is useful in destroying that credulity which tends to control the actions of the simple-minded, for when lies are very obvious they carry their own refutation. The Press as it is, however, is not altogether either good or bad; and on the whole it serves a useful purpose in international politics. Apart from the spreading of information, the Press corrects some of the defects of diplomacy: for diplomacy seldom derives its opinions from the people and seldom addresses the people. The journalist correspondent abroad, on the other hand, can be an unofficial and popular diplomat.[1] He may be used by statesmen or political parties to popularise their policies;[2] and he may be very much

[1] *cf.* Blowitz' "Memoirs," for an interesting, if egoistic, account of a foreign correspondent's life.

[2] Dillon, "Peace Conference." Dr. Dillon gives indications of his being used by the reactionary Russian parties in Paris in order to oppose the Prinkipo suggestion.

feared by those who carry on their designs in secret.[1] The journalist is often a more capable thinker on international issues than the official diplomat and the opinion of a skilled journalist is often more powerful in international affairs than that of a politician.[2] In France the journalist has a direct entry into politics and the French Press is strong in its views of foreign policy especially.[3]

The number of periodical publications in the world at present is said to be about 72,000 ; but that is probably an underestimate. There is an International Press Association which has so far only considered the danger of false or misleading news. There is also an International Congress for Periodicals which held meetings in 1910 and 1912 : and the Press is affected by an international arrangement of May 4th, 1910, for preventing the circulation of indecent literature.

The first important fact in regard to the Press in international politics is that its characteristics are similar in every country. There is a classification of the Press which cuts across national or governmental frontiers and unites all the Socialist and Radical papers of all countries, dividing them from all the Conservative and Militarist papers. This is important because in every country the Press of one colour chiefly relies on the foreign Press of the same colour in order to show that its view of international affairs is correct. Thus militarist organs like the *Morning Post* can find much to prove that Germany is arming in the *Deutsche Tägeszeitung*, and on the other hand a Socialist paper in one country can show that Socialism is progressing abroad by using chiefly foreign Socialist organs. Again, the Press of the Conservative type is allied in every country with large financial interests. This is particularly the case with the French Press. Certain French banks are said to pay regular monthly sums to the chief French papers which are, as it were, retaining fees, and in consideration

[1] Nevinson's articles in *Harpers'*, afterwards republished as " A Modern Slavery," revealed disagreeable facts.

[2] If one may count them journalists chiefly, Mr. Norman Angell in his " Great Illusion " did more than many diplomatists to set men thinking : great numbers of copies have been read in every civilised country : Mr. Brailsford in his " War of Steel and Gold " has advanced the subject ; and Mr. Seton Watson has assisted in destroying an Empire.

[3] Clemenceau, Pichon and Tardieu were all journalists. The *Temps* is usually regarded as the voice of the Foreign Office. *cf.* article in French Supplement to *Times*, September 6, 1919.

of which the communiqués of the banks on new issues or on conditions in trade are inserted in the papers without any sign of their source. This is not a secret system, and several agencies exist for placing the banks' views in the proper journals : but obviously it has a very important bearing on the raising of loans by the attractions offered to the small investor. In a similar manner financial papers in Great Britain are said to be in close connection with particular financial groups. But apart from special connections it is obvious that papers giving information as to investments will naturally be read by those who possess some wealth and will naturally also emphasize what is likely to be of interest to those classes. Policy is not necessarily or mainly financial in its purpose; but clearly there is a connection between the news given of a foreign country and the position of the national trade or investments in that country. Again, there is a natural similarity of policy among all those in every country who stand for the established system.

Apart, however, from the action of each section of the national Press upon the opinions of that nation, there are a few papers which have an international status. The *Times* of London and the *Temps* of Paris may be said to affect opinion outside England and France, although less and less as education progresses, because of the tradition that they stand more closely in relation to their Governments than do other papers.

In connection with the Press are the great News Agencies —Reuter's, Havas, Wolff's, and the Associated Press of America. These are large financial enterprises and their agents are, therefore, naturally prone to take or at any rate to promulgate news of a particular colour. It is not that they misrepresent facts : such misrepresentation may occur ; but facts are so many and various that it is always easy to adjust them to the support of particular opinions. The point is that selection is absolutely necessary and the unconscious criterion by reference to which the news agencies work is the criterion accepted by the governing and capital-owning classes. There is, further, an international arrangement by which, for example, the foreign agencies derive their French news from Havas : so that Reuter's news of France and the Associated Press news and Wolff's are all the same. The connection of the agencies with governmental sources of information in each

INTERNATIONAL POLITICS OF THE DAILY PRESS.

	Belgium.	France.	Spain.	Germany.
Socialist ..	Peuple. Voriut.	Humanité.	Socialista.	Freiheit.
Radical ..	—	Dépêche de Toulouse.	Pais. Progresso.	Vorwärts. Münchener Post.
Liberal ..	Indépendance Belge. Etoile Belge.	Petite République.	Diario Universal. Imparcial.	Berliner Tageblatt. Frankfurter Zeitung.
Conservative ..	Libre Belgique. Journal de Bruxelles.	Journal des Debats. Temps.	Epoca.	Täglishe Rundschau.
Militarist ..	Nation Belge.	Matin. Action Française.	Acción. A.B.C.	Deutsche Tagezeitung Die Post.

	Great Britain.	Italy.	U.S.A.
Socialist ..	Herald.	Avanti.	The Call (N.Y.)
Radical ..	Daily News. Manchester Guardian.	Secolo. Stampa.	World (N.Y.)
Liberal ..	Westminster Gazette.	Corriere della sera (Milan).	Evening Post (N.Y.)
Conservative ..	Daily Telegraph. Times.	Giornale d'Italia.	New York Times.
Militarist ..	Daily Mail. Morning Post.	Idea Nazionale.	Tribune (N.Y.)

country is natural ; for the correspondent wishes to be on good terms with so good a source as a foreign office and a foreign office is not averse to using a correspondent.

For example, Reuter's agent in Japan having been concerned in disagreeable revelations as to bribery by armament firms, Reuter now has Japanese news from an unimpeachable Japanese source, the Japanese National News Agency, which is practically governmental.[1] Again, the German Government before the war joined with certain large firms in the German export trade to found a syndicate for influencing the Press in foreign countries in the German interest.[2] Wolff's Telegraphic-Bureau was to supply all the German news and it was intended to enter into agreements with the Agence Havas and with Reuter's to supply German news only if derived from Wolff's.

In addition to the agencies, all great newspapers have their own correspondents abroad and these have been often persons of consequence in the diplomatic world. The foreign correspondent of a great newspaper may be used as a mouthpiece by a foreign government or a foreign political party, as for example the Kaiser used the *Daily Telegraph* correspondent in his " interview." The chief purpose, however, of the foreign correspondent is to correct or supplement the information supplied by the agencies ; and obviously each paper of a definite political colour must have some person abroad who can see that colour or at least is not colour-blind. It may be taken for granted that no educated reader now believes in the existence of a distinction between news and views : the conception of perfectly colourless views is absurd and indeed the most effective inculcation of views is effected by the publication of statements of fact rather than by expressions of opinion. Statements are not proved untrue if statements of many kinds appear ; since facts are infinite in number and publication depends upon selection.

It is recognised that the international activities of the

---

[1] The " correction " of news from an agency is not always made at the source. The representative of a certain agency in Russia (who must remain nameless) has revealed that of his telegrams 50 per cent. were stopped by the British Admiralty, another 25 per cent. by his own Central Office, and about 20 per cent. of the remainder by the newspapers themselves. The remaining 5 per cent. hardly gave his original view of the situation.

[2] Particulars are given in *Cd.* 7595, Sept., 1914. The essential facts were published in the *Deutsche Export Revue*, June 5, 1914.

Press could be more useful and less harmful: and it is well known that certain groups of papers aim at warfare and trade for the armaments industry.[1] Krupps actually own or control the *Rheinische Westfaelische Zeitung*, the *Tägliche Rundschau* and the *Neueste Nachrichten*. But the suggestion of reform by instituting a governmental or official organ savours of the simplicity of mind of the Abbé St. Pierre. Nothing is to be gained by substituting governmental for private manipulation of public opinion; but clearly there might be a very useful co-ordination of the Press groups in all countries which are capable of understanding and expressing the international mind.

Solutions based upon a conflict of foreign policies will but create problems still more difficult to solve. The problems of international politics must be solved by the adoption of an international attitude for their solution: and on that attitude will be based a policy implying that all groups have something to gain from that solution. This does not require any benevolent altruism or self-sacrifice of one nation for the sake of another, although such heights of virtue may be best: but even enlightened selfishness should prove that an international policy is necessary in the modern world.

The world of international politics contains sufficient evidence in the results of the great war to warrant the belief in the urgent need for a development of this international mind. After the dissolution of the Austro-Hungarian Empire the Austrian Republic was without coal or adequate food supplies for Vienna. At the end of the summer of 1919 the Republic entered into an agreement with the Czech Government at Prague for the supply of coal, and 6,000 trucks left Austria for Czecho-Slovakia: but the coal in November was not forthcoming. There were supplies of food in Trieste which could have been brought to Vienna, but they did not move. The Entente representatives had seriously and quite honestly promised help; but the administrative machine was overloaded and worked slowly. The consequence was death and starvation in Austria. What was the fundamental cause of the difficulty? The state-structure left by the Peace Treaty. Austria was forbidden to unite with Germany

---

[1] "The World's Press," 1914, issued by Sell, has an article by Dr. A. H. Fried on the organisation of the Press for peace purposes: but it is indefinite.

and separated from the new states bordering her. The goods would not move because there was no unifying administrative machine including under it both the producers and the consumers of the goods, and the Republic was too weak and isolated to exercise pressure against the other Governments concerned.[1]

The efforts of private benevolence were sufficient only for sending small supplies of foodstuffs and medical stores for the use of the children and the diseased.[2] The hospitals in Vienna indeed throughout the war had formed a bulwark for Western Europe against the advancing tides of cholera and plague from the East; and therefore while the West was starving the people of Vienna the scientists of the same city were serving the West. The hospitals after the armistice were in part repaid the debt of gratitude by private scientific and medical assistance; but the situation became increasingly worse throughout the autumn of 1919. It is true that Vienna had lived upon an Imperialism which absorbed into itself before the war the vitality and wealth of subject races in Bohemia and elsewhere, and therefore the Viennese middle and official classes were suffering for wrongs formerly done for their advantage if not on their decision: but the problem was not one of punishing culprits or permitting a natural retribution. The international problem arises from the interdependence of nations; for disease and disorder in Vienna involve disease and disorder in other states, and therefore the situation demanded not a balancing of rival interests in the foreign policies of various nations, but a genuine international view as a basis for a genuine international policy. Either joint action of many governments or the action of one government as an agent of international interests might be necessary; but the important point was not so much the machinery as the force to move it. That force could only be a public opinion operative in the international sphere; and that was lacking.

Another indication of the circumstances now prevailing may be found in the history of inter-allied war controls. At the beginning of the war the Allies were purchasing food supplies separately in the American market, and it

---

[1] *cf.* an admirable article, "Die Ursachen der Brot und Kohlenkrise," in the *Arbeiter-Zeitung*, November 21. The same number announced the closing down of industries and the stoppage of trains in Vienna.

[2] *cf.* Cmd. 641 (1920) Reports on British Relief Missions.

was found that they were putting up the price against one another. Therefore joint purchase was adopted. A system of governmental controls grew up: private traders in the several countries were displaced by the governments and the several governments were allocated supplies from those jointly purchased by inter-ally organisations such as the Wheat Commission, the Sugar Commission and the so-called Executives for Meat, Oils and Fats, etc. Finally in 1918 the tonnage problem became so acute that the Allied Maritime Transport Council was established: and this controlled the ships of allied nations and was able to affect even neutral shipping. The Council was for a time an inter-ally body with a genuine international control, used indeed for war purposes but based upon the international plan of distributing the available resources among the nations concerned with regard to the needs of the populations and not in deference to the comparative wealth and power of the several groups. The feeling of common interest in war was enough to support this extreme instance of governmental control over economic forces.

At the Armistice the whole system of controls began to dissolve. It was no longer necessary for ships to sail in convoy, munitions ceased to take up freight-space and every day there was less pull on available transport for non-commercial needs. The Allied Maritime Transport Council ceased to operate: and the national controls were relaxed. The United States particularly was unwilling to continue war measures in which as the sellers her citizens had to receive less from an international joint purchase than they could get in an open and competitive market. From November 1918 to January 1919 no provision was made to substitute for the older controls some new system: but in January a Council of Supply and Relief was created which used the organisation for relieving Belgium in order to relieve Eastern Europe. This, however, was obviously inadequate; and a Supreme Economic Council was established,[1] under which the Relief Council acted as an international Food control; and new Commissions were appointed to reorganise transport in Poland and other such countries. The Supreme Economic Council, acting under the Armistice agreement, sold to Germany about

[1] Members were France, Great Britain, U.S.A., Italy and, for some time, Belgium. It may be noted that Japan did not belong to any of the international bodies, either of the war or after.

700,000 tons of foodstuffs between April and August 1919. Since the signing of the Treaty, however, the Supreme Economic Council has been without a representative of the United States and it has attempted to deal with the food supplies of the late Allies only. Commissions still continued to operate in reorganising transport in Eastern Europe and distributing some supplies; and joint purchase of meat and some other foods was continued on a limited scale. But the pre-war economic organisation was reviving: the interests of private traders were more strongly organised and it may be that the time had really passed for governmental action.

The practical problems are not simple. First, there can be no effective international joint purchase or control unless the several Governments control their own nationals and "play fair." Secondly, every government appeals to an international body when it stands to gain, and no government is likely to maintain an international body of which it bears all the burdens without benefit to itself. Thirdly, every government is amenable to political pressure from strong groups of its own nationals. Fourthly, international confidence cannot survive if the governments gaining from international action use that gain for militarist and economic ends.

There are not, however, only two possibilities, one governmental international control and the other private competition in an open market in which the wealthy groups take all the available resources. There might be an international organisation of foodstuffs, material and transport for the public service of the populations, independently of government purchase and of private profit-making. There might be international co-operative trade. But only a strong public opinion, using intellectual and imaginative ability in an international public service, could establish and develop such a system: and that international mind is lacking.

There are, of course, many who desire to leave the world better than they found it: and in international politics they recognise the problems and they know that the common life of men will not advance in happiness so long as national war and private greed are so prominent as they now are. Idealists they may be called. Idealists are the salt of the earth: but the salt is still in the salt-cellar, it has not been put into the eatables, and salt is

UNOFFICIAL INTERNATIONAL ORGANISATIONS

after all for seasoning, not for snaring birds, as some politicians seem to suppose. The problem, therefore, is to make ideals effective and to induce idealists to act in financial, commercial and administrative affairs.

The creation of the international mind and the organisation of international action in every sphere, governmental and voluntary, is therefore the greatest need of the world to-day. The need of the world is indeed shown in the desire of men, women and children for justice, liberty and all those other goods which go to the make of happiness: but the majority do not understand what is involved when they desire peace and bread and boots. International politics, if they heard of it, would seem to them a very abstract interest of specialists, as peace has been made to appear to them an unaccountable desire of cranks. It is a world, then, of blind desire for goods, the enjoyment of which is made impossible by the actions of those very persons who desire them.

BIBLIOGRAPHY

Books of Reference.[1]

Annuaire de la Vie Internationale, 1908–1909, 1910–1911, Brussels.

Almanach de Gotha: Annual. Justus Perthes.

Statesman's Year-Book. Annual. Macmillan, London.

The Peace Year-Book: Annual. London. National Peace Council.

Angell, Norman. The Great Illusion. Heinemann. First published, 1909.

Bourgeois, Emile. Manuel historique de politique étrangère. 3 vols. (General history of the old type, strongly French in outlook.)

Brailsford, H. N. War of Steel and Gold. Bell. 9th Edition. 1917.

Brailsford, H. N. A League of Nations. Swarthmore Press. First Edition. 1917.

Burns, C. Delisle. The Morality of Nations. London University Press, 1915.

Carnegie Endowment. Report on Balkan Wars. 1913.

Culbertson, W. S. Commercial Policy. Appleton & Co. New York. 1919.

Debidour, A. Histoire diplomatique de l'Europe. Vol. I, 1814–1848: Vol. II, 1848–1890; Vol. III, 1878–1904; Vol. III, Second Part, 1904–1915 (published in 1917). Paris. Alcan.

Dickinson, G. L. The Choice before us. 1918. Allen and Unwin. (A review of militarism and international policy.)

Dickinson, G. L. The European Anarchy. Allen and Unwin. 1916.

Foster, J. W. The Practice of Diplomacy. Boston. 1906. (Chiefly American.)

Girault, A. Colonial Tariff Policy of France. Oxford. 1916. Carnegie Endowment.

---

[1] Books on the several countries will be found in the bibliographies in the *Statesman's Year-Book*.

BIBLIOGRAPHY

Greenwood, A., and others. Introduction to the study of International Relations. Macmillan. (Essays on Law, Economics, Subject Races, etc., by various authors.)

Goschen, Viscount. Theory of Foreign Exchanges. 1910. Effingham Wilson. London.

Hawtrey, R. G. Currency and Credit. 1920. Longmans (esp. ch. IV, VI, VII, on Foreign Exchanges).

Heatley, D. P. Diplomacy and the study of International Relations. Oxford Press. 1920.

Herbert, S. Nationality and its Problems. Methuen. 1920.

Higgins, A. P. The Hague Peace Conferences (1909. Cambridge Univ. Press). (The Conventions and Notes.)

Hanotaux, Gabriel. Etudes Diplomatiques. Three series. (1) 1907-1911. La politique de l'equilibre (2) 1912-1913. La guerre des Balkans. (3) War diplomacy. Short sketches of current diplomatic problems. Le Traité de Versailles (1919). (An extreme example of the worst form of the French politics of domination.)

Hobson, C. K. Export of Capital. Constable. 1915.

Hobson, J. A. International Trade.

Holdich, Sir T. H. Political frontiers. Macmillan. 1916.

Keynes, J. M. Economic consequences of the Peace Treaty. Macmillan. Dec., 1919

Lawrence, T. J. The Principles of International Law. Macmillan.

Lysis. Contre l'Oligarchie financière en France. 11th Edit. 1915. Paris, Michel. (A review of the raising of foreign loans in France.)

Oppenheim, L. F. L. International law. 2 vols. Longmans. 1912.

Otlet, Paul. Les problèmes internationaux de la guerre. 1916. (Very general review of international affairs.)

Paish, Sir G. A Permanent League of Nations. Fisher Unwin, 1918. (A short study, chiefly economic.)

Phillimore, Sir W. G. F. Three Centuries of Treaties of Peace. Murray. 1917.

Ponsonby, A. Democracy and Diplomacy. Methuen. 1915.

Pooley, A. M. Secret Memoirs of Count Hayashi. Nash, 1915.

Reinsch, Paul. Public International Unions.

Reinsch, Paul. World Politics at the end of the XIXth Century, as influenced by the Oriental situation. Macmillan. 1900.

Salvemini, G., and others. Come Siamo andati in Libia. Florence. 1914.

Satow, Sir E. A Guide to Diplomatic Practice. 2 vols. Longmans. 1917. (Details of the form of diplomatic communications.)

Tardieu, André. La France et les Alliances. Paris. 1908. Eng. Trans. Macmillan. 1909.

Vissering, G. International Economic and Financial Problems. Macmillan. 1920.

Withers, Hartley. International Finance. Smith Elder. 1916.

Woolf, L. S. International Government. Allen and Unwin. July, 1916.

Woolf, L. S. Empire and Commerce in Africa. Allen and Unwin. 1920.

Woolf, L. S. The future of Constantinople. Allen and Unwin. 1916.

Official Publications.

Federal Trade Commission, U.S.A. Report on Co-operation in American Export Trade. 2 parts. 1916. Washington.

Colonial Office Reports, periodically on various Colonies.

Foreign Office Reports, periodically on various foreign countries and their dependencies, by Consular Officers.

Documents Diplomatiques. Ministère des affaires étrangères. Paris: periodically.

International Labour Office: Report on various labour problems, periodically.

Periodicals.

Revue des sciences politiques. Paris. Ecole libre des sciences politiques. Monthly: 19 fr. p.a.

The New Europe: weekly, 6d. Editor and Proprietor, R. W. Seton-Watson.

Contemporary Review: Appendix of *Facts and Documents*. Monthly.

Political Review of the Foreign Press, and the

Economic Review of the Foreign Press. *Weekly*, 1s. 99, Horseferry Rd., S.W.

INDEX OF SUBJECTS

Abyssinia, 76
Afghanistan, 28
Alby United Company, 102
Allied Maritime Transport, 151, 181
Amalgamated Society of Engineers, 170
Ambassadors, 122
Andorra, 28
Anglo-Persian Oil Company, 79, 98
Anti-Slavery Society, 165
Arbitration, 25, 146
Argentine, 49, 53, 110
Armaments, 132
Armenians, 42
Armstrongs, 134
Attaché, 122, 125
Australia, 39, 50, 51
Austria, 47, 179

Balance of Power, 9, 21, 140
Balkans, 23
Balkan Wars, 24, 135
Baltic States, 23
Banks, 96
Belgian Congo, 60
Belgium, 19
Bill of Exchange, 95
Boxer Rising, 39
Brazil, 49, 93
British Empire, 29 *note*, 153
British North Borneo, 63

Cammell Laird, 135
Capital Abroad, 100
Canada, 47, 51, 171
Catholicism, 40
Centrum Party, 41
Chartered Companies, 55
China, 39, 68, 147
Colombia, 56, 102
Combines, 107
Commercial Treaty, 94

Concert of Europe, 128
Condominium, 150 *note*
Conferences, 128
Congo, 60, 64
Constantinople, 131
Consuls, 123, 126
Controls, 181
Conventions, 129
Corporation of Bondholders, 81
Currency, 83, 93
Czecho-Slovakia, 23, 26

Danube Commission, 150
Dardanelles, 131
Democracy, 140
Department of Overseas Trade, 122
Diplomacy, 8, 118
Dogger Bank, 146 *note*
Drago Doctrine, 25

Egypt, 37, 73, 82
Emigration, 45
England, *see* United Kingdom
Epidemics, 150, 166
Esthonia, 23
Exchange, 92, 99

Federal Reserve Act, 97
Finance, 96
Food Prices, 114
Foreign Offices, 119
Foreign Policy, 5
Foreign Trade, 84
Forestal Company, 105
France, 16, 75, 85, 120, 130
Free Trade, 91
French West Africa, 57
Friends' Emergency, 167

Germany, 41, 100, 130
Gold Coast, 57
Great Britain, *see* United Kingdom

Great Powers, 9, 14, 144
Greece, 23

Hague Conference, 20, 145
Hague Conventions, 25, 27
Havas Agency, 176
Health Bureau, 150
Holland, see Netherlands

Imperialism, 10
India, 44
International Association for Labour Legislation, 164
International Controls, 181
International Maritime Committee, 164
International Labour Movement, 167
International Labour Organisation—
  Conference, 51, 159
  Office, 158
International Law, 144
International Unions, 147
International Rail Syndicate, 107
Inter-parliamentary Union, 165
Ireland, 18, 37
Ironfounders, 171
Islam, 43
Italo-Turkish War, 74
Italy, 19, 36, 38, 47, 74, 130

Japan, 15, 20, 29, 70, 72
Judaism, 42

Kalifate, 45
Korea, 72, 146 *note*
Krupps, 137, 179

Labour Movement, 52, 167
Latvia, 23
League of Nations, 19, 151
Lever Bros., 103
Liberia, 38 *note*
Libya, 75
Luxemburg, 20

Manchuria, 80
Mandates, 156, 165
Marquesas, 65
Meat Combine, 109
Mesopotamia, 98
Metal-buying Combine, 108

Mexico, 71
Middle Ages, 7
Ministry of Labour, 125
Mohammedans, 43
Monaco, 28
Morocco, 73, 65
Mozambique Company, 105
Munroe Doctrine, 26

Nationalism, 37, 85
Nationality, 34
Native Races Bureau, 165
Netherlands, 85
News Agencies, 176
Nicaragua, 28
Norway, 16, 22

Oman, 29
Open Door, 10, 65
Opium, 147
Ottoman Public Debt, 81
Palestine, 43
Panama, 28, 29, 131
Pan-American Union, 25
Pan-Islam, 37
Pan-Turanianism, 37 *note*
Peace Commissions, 25
Peonage, 62
Peru, 62, 165
Peruvian Amazon Company, 62
Poland, 23, 166
Portugal, 60
Portuguese Africa, 58
Postal Union, 149
Press, 174
Protection, 91
Protocol, 129
Putumayo, 62

Races, 38
Racial Minorities, 18, 36
Railway Dividends, 56
Railway Freight Bureau, 149
Red Cross, 166
Religion, 39
Reuter, 176
Rosario, 103
Russia, 23, 32, 69

Scandinavia, 22
Schneider and Company, 137
Secret Treaties, 75, 129
Serb-Croat-Slovene State, 23
Shell Company, 107

INDEX OF SUBJECTS

Shipping, 111
Silesia, 35
Small States, 21
South America, 24, 104
Sovereignty, 31
Soviet Government, 169
Spain, 16, 26, 40
Straits, 131
Suez, 73, 131
Supreme Economic Council, 181
Sweden, 22
Switzerland, 16, 19

Tariffs, 65, 89
Trade, 84
Trade Fluctuation, 112
Treaties, 94, 129, 131
Tripoli, 44, 74
Turkey, 44, 131
Tyrol, 36

United Kingdom, 50, 85, 87, 91, 100, 118, 130
United States, 16, 26, 38, 47, 51, 90, 97, 120, 140
United States Steel Corporation, 106
Universal Postal Union, 149
Upper Silesia, 35

Vatican, 40
Verona Congress, 26
Versailles Treaty, 27
Vickers, 70, 134
Vienna Congress, 10
Vienna, Food Conditions, 180

War, 141, 144
Wolff's Bureau, 179

Zambesia Mining Company, 104

Wyman & Sons Ltd., Printers, London, Reading and Fakenham.